Aquachile

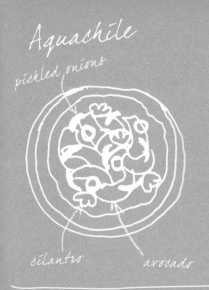

pickled onions

cilantro

avocado

Lamb

lamb shank

pureé

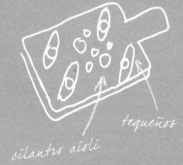

tequeños

cilantro aioli

Cachapitos

queso guayanos

corn cakes

Pabellon

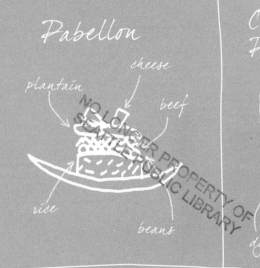

cheese

plantain

beef

rise

beans

Cuban Style Pork Sandwich

pickles

pork belly

dijon

bread

Pulpo Empañadas

empañadas

red churri

Asado Negro Sliders

slaw

asado negro

Three in the Pot

mint

chocolate dirt

vanilla ice cream

avocado chocolate mousse

THE HOMEMADE CHEF

THE HOMEMADE CHEF

ORDINARY INGREDIENTS FOR EXTRAORDINARY FOOD

James

TAHHAN

A CELEBRA BOOK

CELEBRA

Published by New American Library,
an imprint of Penguin Random House LLC
375 Hudson Street, New York, New York 10014

This book is an original publication of New American Library.

First Printing, September 2016

For more information about Penguin Random House, visit penguin.com.

LIBRARY OF CONGRESS CATALOGING-IN-PUBLICATION DATA:
NAMES: JAMES, CHEF, 1988– AUTHOR.
TITLE: THE HOMEMADE CHEF: ORDINARY INGREDIENTS FOR EXTRAORDINARY FOOD/JAMES TAHHAN.
DESCRIPTION: NEW YORK, NEW YORK: NEW AMERICAN LIBRARY, AN IMPRINT OF PENGUIN RANDOM HOUSE,
LLC, 2016. | "A CELEBRA BOOK."
IDENTIFIERS: LCCN 2016000676 (PRINT) | LCCN 2016012685 (EBOOK) | ISBN 9781101990414 |
ISBN 9781101990452 (EBOOK)
SUBJECTS: LCSH: COOKING. | LCGFT: COOKBOOKS.
CLASSIFICATION: LCC TX714 .J355 2016 (PRINT) | LCC TX714 (EBOOK) | DDC 641.5—DC23
LC RECORD AVAILABLE AT HTTP://LCCN.LOC.GOV/2016000676

Printed in China
10 9 8 7 6 5 4 3 2 1

Designed by Pauline Neuwirth

Penguin
Random
House

Mainly to my mother for her relentless support, for urging me to
always do my best, and for giving me all she had,
which nowadays means the world. Thank you.

To Russel Conde for being my pillar of support and guide
who drove me to pursue this magical career, giving me the
confidence to become a chef and do it well.

And to all of you who follow me on TV, social networks, and constantly
visit my restaurants. Without your support,
none of this would be possible.

They say the kitchen is the heart of the
home, and so it must be kept beating
with good flavors and aromas.

contents

THE HOMEMADE CHEF

introduction: welcome!

Dear Reader: Welcome to my first cookbook. Before we get started, I want to congratulate you for deciding to learn more about this beautiful art known as cooking. With each page, we will embark on an adventure that will satisfy your appetite for knowledge, as well as for mouthwatering, fast, healthy dishes. The recipes in this book are inspired by the same dishes I cook at my restaurant, Sabores by Chef James, and at home. Growing up in Venezuela, I fell in love with food through Latin cuisine. As a person with a multicultural background, I'm passionate about combining Latin flavors and cooking methods with different international ingredients that are simple yet anything but ordinary. The result is extraordinary Pan-Latin dishes that have my signature WOW factor—quick, simple, yet sophisticated touches—that will impress your family and friends as well as allow you to master invaluable prepping and cooking skills that you can use for the rest of your life. Whether you're a beginner or you have more experience, I promise you will have fun and be surprised with what you will discover through the joys of cooking. They say the kitchen is the heart of the home, and so it must be kept beating with good flavors and aromas.

For an inexperienced cook, the culinary world can seem intimidating—even complicated—stressful, and intense, but there's actually no reason to fear it. With modern-day advances, cooking has become more simplified. We live in a time when modern kitchen utensils help make our job much easier and most supermarkets carry a huge variety of fresh, high-quality ingredients. When in doubt, we can refer to the Internet and social networks for answers to our questions.

Throughout my career, I have had the opportunity to travel around the world, and this has allowed me to experience the countries I visit through their foods. I like to try typical dishes when I go out to eat, whether the restaurant is well-known or small, or just a food stand on the street (and many of them are amazing). I befriend the locals and get their recommendations on where to eat, which I follow to the letter. Although some recommendations aren't all that great, most of them are 100 percent worth it. On many occasions, I have had better meals at small, intimate, local spots than at more high-end restaurants. This goes to show that cooking well is within everyone's reach. You don't need a big kitchen, just the right attitude and a little creativity.

My own story shows that if you want to cook, or achieve anything you set your mind to, all you need is the desire to do so. When I arrived in the United States with my mother, I was only fourteen years old, and our start here, like that of most immigrants, was far from easy. We lived in a small house, and although the kitchen was also small, I used it to prepare easy meals. My mother was working up to four jobs to provide for us, and when I saw her efforts, I decided to pitch in by getting a job. Although at that young age I already had an interest in cooking, it wasn't my priority. My main goal at the time was to study and work to get ahead in life.

In those days, my routine was simple: school then work. And, boy, did I work! Before becoming a chef, I sold cell phones at a small stand in a shopping mall; I was so young that working at my age was considered illegal, but I figured out a way to convince the owner to hire me. I later sold vitamins and shortly thereafter jumped into telemarketing. Just when I thought I'd stay in the industry, I was offered the chance to make radio commercials, so I decided to move into the social communications world. Meanwhile, I was studying chemistry so I could become a dentist (can you imagine me as a dentist?!), and as I was finishing my degree, I realized I was incredibly curious about cooking, so I decided to register at a culinary institute to follow my calling as a chef.

To this day, I still find what followed surprising. One day, while I was conducting some interviews on the radio to cover a culinary event, I was invited to television network Telemundo to speak about the event. When I arrived, there had been a setback and the Telemundo reps said they wouldn't be able to air my segment. Just as I was leaving, a producer asked me if I was a real chef and if I could cook. Since I had already finished my culinary studies, I said yes, and he asked me to meet with him the following day for an interview to become the network's next chef. I said I'd be there, but just to get him out of my way so I could wrap up everything else I still had to get done that day. When the day of the interview came along, I didn't go because I had to work; however, before heading out to my job, I got a call from my boss, who said I had to go to Telemundo because the producer was bothering him and asking that he let me do the interview. To make a long story short, when I arrived at Telemundo studios, I discovered that I was the only one dressed in business attire because the "interview" was actually a cooking demonstration! I managed to wing it by asking the other chefs if I could borrow their utensils to participate in this test. Against all odds, I was able to land the position, and I am grateful to have been welcomed into your homes.

> If you want to cook or achieve anything you set your mind to, all you need is the desire to do so.

Every day, I wake up and think about how lucky I am to have been able to follow my dream and, above all, to cook for people, especially because my interest in the kitchen began unexpectedly. Yet that's how life surprises us.

It all started with the help of a charismatic neighbor I always admired: Señor David. As a child in Venezuela, I would go to his house and play with his children, so much so that sometimes I spent more time at their house than at my own. After my first few visits, I quickly discovered that Señor David was an exceptional chef and that while his children did not like eating the delicacies he prepared, I loved them. That forged a deep bond between us: He found someone who enjoyed his cooking as much as he did, and I discovered a real passion at an early age. I still remember the first dish we prepared together: *perlitas a la andaluza* (Andalusian pearls), or small fried fish. I felt like a real chef as I breaded and fried the little fish. I remember they were so small that we could eat them whole, with bones and all, and the flavor . . . incredible.

Because of these great experiences I've had with food, I'm always surprised by the reasons why many people don't cook—from lack of time to the usual "I'm not good at it." Yet nothing could be further from the truth. That's why, since the beginning of my culinary education, I've made it my mission to make cooking accessible, enjoyable, and a natural process for everyone. This goal led me to simplify the way I explain cooking, so that it's easy to understand no matter how much experience you've had in the kitchen. I take a very direct approach: Easier explanations lead to better outcomes. Once you start, you'll soon notice this at home. You'll see that cooking is more than following a recipe. Cooking is a philosophy—a little bit of this, a little less of that; they're all decisions that will come intuitively while you cook and develop your own culinary philosophy.

It's okay to make mistakes. We all make them, and that's how we learn!

My first objective with this book is to speak the language that comes naturally to me, a language that transcends all cultures—the language of food. My second goal is to bring the concept of uncomplicated cooking—which I practice regularly in my cooking shows—to your home. I will take you by the hand and slowly guide you through this process, showing you what ingredients to use and how to buy them, what utensils each kitchen needs, and how to make amazing dishes at home, with the easiest methods, as if you were a professional chef. Between recipes and tips, I will also share my own experiences when I first started to learn how to cook. You will discover several of my cooking secrets, which will come in very handy at home, as well as some of the slipups I've had while cooking, to show that it's okay to make mistakes. After all, to have that "wow factor" that I often mention on TV, the first ingredient every recipe must include is fun, which is of course followed by passion.

In this book, I've also included essential and simple skills that will make your life much easier in the kitchen. You'll learn basic knife skills such as trimming fat from primal cuts without sacrificing the meat's flavor or texture. Likewise, I will share basic boiling and simmering techniques and how to use them to maximize your time. We can't forget that high-quality ingredients enhance the flavor of everything you make. That's why I've also dedicated a section to seasonal ingredients, the benefits of buying organic produce, how to choose primal cuts based on the dish you will be making, and even how to test for freshness when buying fish and seafood.

As for the recipes, I've included mainly dishes that are easy to make but do not sacrifice flavor, so that you can prepare delicious food without spending too much time in the kitchen. You'll also find nutritious recipes that don't take away from your diet and instead introduce more food through a variety of healthy ingredients.

Although a larger kitchen space and the latest equipment and gadgets can make our lives easier, it's not necessary to have both to enjoy making these meals. To prove that, I've included tips on alternative ways to prepare recipes with the utensils at hand so that you can take full advantage of what you have. When I had just moved to the United States, I had to cook in one of the smallest kitchens I've ever seen in my life, so I can assure you that if you follow my directions, you'll be able to do a great job in your kitchen.

Finally, this book would not be complete without including some of my favorite cocktails, which will liven up any gathering or event. Even though the kitchen is the

heart of the home and food is what keeps it beating, we must also have drinks now and then to add a little more spice.

My main purpose in writing this book is to provide you with the only skills you'll ever need to cook with confidence. I've zeroed in on the most important lessons and tips I acquired during my time in culinary school and as a chef in my own restaurant to make cooking easy for anyone. I want you to feel confident enough to try something new and spontaneous in the comfort of your own kitchen. I also want you to have the information you need to make your own decisions and to be able to pass on that knowledge—including where to shop, what ingredients to use, and how to prepare them—to your family and friends. My goal is to get you excited about discovering more of this marvelous world, so that you can turn ordinary ingredients into extraordinary dishes. I hope to inspire you to have faith in homemade cooking, so that you can go to a restaurant, see the ingredients, and make a better version at home, encouraging you to treat and nurture yourself with an exquisite dish that you were able to make in just a few minutes. Together we will overcome whatever intimidates you in your kitchen, and you will soon realize that you are capable of cooking anything you set out to make.

the heart of the home: the kitchen

Get ready to turn your kitchen into a place where you feel most at ease. The kitchen is an area of absolute freedom, so you must treat it as such. In this creative space, you can do whatever you want, because the only fixed rules when it comes to mixing flavors, textures, and aromas are set by you and your palate.

The first step to creating extraordinary food is to make sure the kitchen is well stocked. Nothing's worse than wanting to satisfy a craving and realizing you don't have the ingredients you need to prepare what you want. I don't wish this on anyone! Besides having to go to the supermarket hungry, you'll end up buying more than you need and will waste precious time you don't have. That's why, every day, I like to make sure my kitchen is fully equipped.

Now, when I say this, I'm referring to a simple yet necessary list of ingredients and utensils you must have handy at all times to cook delicious dishes with ease—and to ensure that you won't be left with unsatisfied cravings. Don't worry; these necessities are easy to get, pretty affordable, and, most important, very useful.

basic list of ingredients

Olive oil: Likely the most essential ingredient on this list. I call it the kitchen's all-in-one because you can use it to dress, marinate, sauté, roast, fry, emulsify, and more. I recommend you buy the extra virgin kind, or organic extra virgin, to get better flavor and fewer chemicals.

Garlic: Key to giving food that extra kick. You can buy it fresh or minced in a jar, though I recommend you always buy it fresh. If it hasn't been peeled yet, it should be kept outside of the fridge; however, if it is peeled, it's best to keep it in the refrigerator.

Onion: A very popular ingredient given its versatility and use in different dishes. It's always good to have red and yellow onions at home since each type provides us with different benefits. Red onion has a spicy note when it's raw; however, when cooked, the flavor is somewhat toned down. That's why this is the type of onion widely used for salsas in Mexico, whereas the yellow onion lacks that strong flavor, and once cooked, the flavor is very light. This is why the yellow onion is widely used in Peru's and Ecuador's ceviche. When you buy onions, make sure they are firm; as you would with garlic, store them in the fridge only if they're peeled.

Chiles: One of my favorite ingredients on earth: colorful and aromatic, with lots of flavor and that typical spiciness that awakens your senses. I've always liked spice, even when I was young, and that's why I think chiles are necessary in every kitchen. There are two types of chiles: fresh and dried. Fresh chiles are smooth and brightly colored, while dried chiles are given more time to ripen and dehydrate, which gives them their wrinkled skin and distinct flavor. The most popular fresh chiles are serrano, jalapeño, and pequin, one of the hottest chiles in the world. As for dried chiles, the most popular are chipotle, chile de arbol, and guajillo.

Given their spicy flavor, they're ideal additions to soups, salsas, and stews and an excellent accompaniment to meats. As they can be very hot, use with caution.

Tomatoes: The base ingredient for countless salsas, stews, and even drinks, such as the popular bloody mary. They're available fresh or canned, diced or pureed. Fresh tomatoes last longer in the fridge; just make sure not to store them for too long, as the cool temperature diminishes their flavor.

Avocados: One of my favorite ingredients given its creaminess and neutral flavor. There are several types of avocados, Hass being the most popular. To test for ripeness, gently press the avocado to see if the skin gives in to the touch. If it doesn't and it feels firm, leave it outside the refrigerator to accelerate the ripening process.

Aromatic herbs: There are many aromatic herbs; however, the basic ones you should always have handy are cilantro, parsley, basil, rosemary, and oregano. As you try out different recipes, you will expand the types of herbs you use, but until you reach that point, these five will suffice.

- **Cilantro:** An indispensable herb given its use for seasoning salsas, soups, and stews. The stems tend to have a stronger flavor than the leaves, but because I like cilantro so much, I use both. Make sure to thoroughly rinse any dirt or debris before using.

- **Parsley:** When you want to add fresh flavor to any dish, parsley is the way to go. You can use it to cook or as a garnish. Its vibrant green color creates a beautiful presentation on a plate.

- **Basil:** Ideal for reinvigorating the flavor of salads, dressings, and sauces. It goes well with tomato and is marvelous in soups and stews. I suggest you use only the leaves because the stem's flavor may be too strong.

- **Rosemary:** A powerful and colorful aromatic, rosemary is a great addition to beans, chicken, and stews. Make sure the leaves aren't yellow and that they don't easily come off the stem. If you refrigerate it, fresh rosemary can last for up to five days.

- **Oregano:** One of the most versatile herbs in the kitchen, oregano can be used to enhance the flavor of all types of meat. It can also be added fresh to pastas and pizzas, and, as if that weren't enough, it gives soups and broths a special touch. You can add a sprig of oregano to a bottle filled with oil or vinegar to aromatize it and later use as dressing.

Smoked paprika: Paprika will give your food a smoky and powerful flavor. It's used to marinate primal cuts and added to soups and broths. You can find sweet, bittersweet, and spicy varieties, although the spicy ones aren't that hot.

Salt: A universal seasoning that should be in every household. Salt is your best ally to enhance any food's flavor, but it's important not to overdo it. If you add too little, it will likely go unnoticed, and you can always add more later, but if you add too much, you'll ruin any dish's flavor. Overall, the level of saltiness depends on a person's preference, so when a recipe calls for the use of salt, season to taste unless the success of the recipe relies on just the right amount of salt, like for baked goods. Also, you will find that there are many varieties of salt, but I prefer sea salt, kosher salt, and *sel gris* (French gray sea salt). Beware of regular salt because it tends to be high in iodine and has a bitter aftertaste.

Pepper: Salt's most loyal companion. Pepper is used mainly to season meats, vegetables, stews, and soups. It's better to buy the peppercorns and grind them with a pepper mill as you need it so that the pepper best maintains its flavor. However, you can also buy ground pepper to save time. Similar to salt, the amount of pepper needed is based on preference unless a recipe calls for a specific amount.

kitchen utensils

Now that you have an idea of what basic ingredients should be in your kitchen, let's explore the utensils that will save you time and make cooking a whole lot easier.

Food processor: We haven't been able to invent a time machine, but a food processor is your best time-saving tool when cooking. Even the most basic machine will help you cut, mix, and puree quickly and effectively, so try to get one for your kitchen.

Knife set: A chef's best friend is his or her knife set. A good set can save you time and effort when cooking. You don't need every type of knife, just these quality essentials: a forged steel chef's knife (with a 10- to 12-inch blade), a kitchen knife (with a 2½- to 3-inch blade), and a serrated knife (with a 6-inch blade). I also recommend you invest in a stone knife sharpener to help you keep your knives at their best for cooking. Caution: Do not sharpen the serrated knife with this stone, as you will ruin the blade.

Nonstick pans: Invest in good-quality nonstick pans—they'll last longer so you don't have to keep buying new ones. The ideal pan should have a thick and heavy iron base and a good nonstick coating. Nothing is more frustrating than having the perfect omelet come undone because it has stuck to the pan. Ideally, the pan should be oven-safe as well and the handle should feel comfortable in your hand. It's worth having different sizes: A small pan is ideal for individual meals; medium and large ones are best for when you are entertaining guests. Check to see that they are free of PFOA (a chemical used in making Teflon). Use wooden spoons, as they are gentler on the pan's surface.

Cutting boards: Made out of sturdy plastic or wood, cutting boards are an essential tool for cutting up meat, vegetables, and fruit. If your budget permits, buy a wooden cutting board. With proper care, it can last a lifetime. For health reasons, it's important to have two boards: one to cut raw meats and the other for fresh produce.

Pots: No matter the size of your kitchen, set aside some space for pots. It's best to have a variety of sizes. A large pot is great to have around since it will help you save time when you want to cook large quantities of food.

Baking dishes: Baking is a healthy alternative to frying. That's why these dishes are a necessity for every kitchen. You can use them to roast meats and poultry, like a huge Thanksgiving turkey, and bake cookies and cakes.

Tongs: A good pair of tongs can save you from many mistakes and burns. They give you better control when grilling food and, of course, they can be used to serve your delicious recipes!

Wooden spoon and fork: Once you've invested in a good set of pots and pans, use utensils that won't ruin them. That's why it's important to have wooden spoons and forks: They don't conduct heat and are easy on your pots and pans.

Mortar and pestle: One of the kitchen utensils I like most since it's used to extract the flavor of countless ingredients, such as garlic, basil, and avocado. It's very easy and fun to use and can also help you create new combinations and flavors.

Strainer: Very useful for washing fruit and vegetables and straining pasta. Nowadays there are beautiful strainers that can add a decorative touch to your kitchen.

Grater: There is a great variety of quality graters available. Make sure you get one that's of good quality so that it stays sharp for a long time and you're able to grate foods like cheese and chocolate effortlessly.

Peeler: This utensil will win you over. Get one with a good handle so that it's easy to hold. It will save you time, energy, and frustration.

tips to make the most of your kitchen space

Turn your kitchen into its own world! It's a phrase I say often on my TV show and to the chefs at my restaurants. I use it for inspiration, and I hope it has the same effect on you at home.

We would all love to cook in a big, comfortable, and spacious kitchen that allows us optimal mobility. And who hasn't dreamed of having one of those incredible kitchens seen on TV where everything looks high-tech and magical? The refrigerator is an immense portal that can cool anything and the ovens are volcanoes capable of cooking meals in mere minutes. As a child, I always dreamed of having this type of kitchen, and it was one of the things that inspired me to become a chef.

Having a spacious kitchen is a luxury more than the norm, and it's not a necessity when it comes to making excellent dishes quickly and effectively. In fact, I don't have a big kitchen at home, but I figured out a way to make it seem more open and comfortable when I cook. The trick is to keep it organized and include items that make it a place you enjoy being in. My kitchen is simple yet pleasing to the eye; it looks normal but has great capabilities. I try to use colors that I like and that complement everything within the space. You may think it's not such an important detail, but it helps inspire me to cook. Reproducing this effect in your home will help you feel like a chef in your own kitchen.

I've cooked in different types of kitchens throughout my career and I can assure you that size does not matter. The only determining factor that will affect the outcome of your dishes is the passion with which you make them. So get ready to turn your kitchen, big or small, into a pleasant space overflowing with flavors and aromas. Here are some tips:

1. *Keep your kitchen organized:* Every kitchen must be organized, especially small ones, so as to make the best use of the space. It's important to keep the utensils that are used together in the same place. Likewise, I recommend you organize your kitchen in order of importance; in other words, keep within arm's reach the things you use the most, and store the utensils and ingredients you use less often on higher shelves of the cabinet. You can also place your most-used utensils in the drawers or cabinets closer to the sink. This will make washing and putting them away more efficient.

2. *Label your drawers:* If you're constantly doing a thousand things at once and don't have time to spare, like me, this tip is very useful. Labeling drawers will save you precious time when you're looking for a particular tool. It can also keep you from messing up other organized spaces. I usually label the drawers where I store ingredients because it helps me put away my groceries faster. Some prefer labeling everything—the places for both ingredients and utensils—it really depends on your needs.

3. *Use storage baskets:* They're a blessing because they help maximize the space in your kitchen by containing loose food items to a specific place, which helps you stay organized. You can place them on lower cabinet shelves and use them to store canned goods and boxes of pasta and cereal.

4. *Take advantage of vertical space:* If you don't have enough horizontal space, then use vertical space. Install bars with hooks on your walls: They'll help you take advantage of the space and will give your kitchen a decorative touch. Use the bars to hang removable accessories, such as paper towels and tongs. For even more convenience, find what you need in a hardware store to make easy vertical shelves to store everything from pots to utensils. You won't have to bend down each time you want to use a pot. Believe me, in the long run it helps!

The only determining factor that will affect the outcome of your dishes is the passion with which you make them.

5. *Organize in towers:* Another way to take advantage of vertical space is to stack plates and plastic containers in towers. It doesn't seem like much, but slowly the inches you save add up and help keep your kitchen well organized.

6. *Maximize cabinet space:* Part of making your small kitchen spacious is creating unconventional places to store accessories. Make better use of your cabinets by adding cabinet door hooks for storing small items. But be careful! Don't hang heavy objects because you could damage the cabinet door. I like using this space to store spices and seasonings, such as salt, pepper, and adobo. They're easily accessible when I need to add a dash of seasoning to a dish.

7. *Be smart about storage:* Many food items come in boxy containers that take up too much space. Here's a very simple solution: Before storing them, get rid of the packaging and simply store the food. If need be, place the food inside an airtight bag to keep it fresh. Tea, cereal, and pastas are good examples of types of food you can store without the packaging. Just make sure to write the expiration date on the bag.

8. *Use multipurpose accessories:* A smart way to gain inches in your kitchen is to use multipurpose utensils. For example, versatile silverware that you can use daily and with guests will save you quite a bit of space. You can do the same if you buy multipurpose corkscrews and can openers. Another option is to buy one measuring cup with different measures rather than a set of individual measuring cups. The same goes for spoons. Buy one that allows you to measure everything with one utensil to save time and space.

9. *Organize your refrigerator:* Use plastic boxes to organize each section by ingredients. Designate the shelves on the door for tall containers, such as beverages and salsas. I also recommend that you place meats and cold cuts in the lower half of the refrigerator and inside containers to avoid spillage and a disastrous mess. It's important that you place fruits and vegetables inside the refrigerator drawers to protect their leaves and skins from the cold. Lastly, try to organize ingredients based on their expiration dates: those closer to expiring must be in the front, while those that will last a little longer can be placed farther back.

10. *Add decoration:* Another trick to visually enlarge your kitchen and make you feel more comfortable is to use neutral and smooth colors. Together with natural light, these colors give smaller rooms a sense of spaciousness. If your kitchen is blue, it doesn't mean you have to completely make it over, but do try to create a peaceful and warm space, a place where you feel comfortable while you're preparing your favorite dishes.

Some tips will work better than others, given your own kitchen's characteristics. You don't have to use them all, just the ones that work for you and best reflect your style. With time, you'll develop your own methods to "enlarge" your kitchen, and you'll be moving around it effortlessly, experiencing the joy of cooking.

en route to fantastic flavors

Throughout my career, I've made countless mistakes in the kitchen, so many that if I tried to list them all in this book, I wouldn't have enough pages. Okay, maybe I'm exaggerating just a little, but my point is that everyone, even the most renowned chefs, makes mistakes.

During one of my first live TV episodes, I was grabbing some vegetables from the oven as I described to the audience their wonderful aroma, when I carelessly set part of the hot tray on my wrist, burning it instantly. However, since the show had to go on, I fought back the urge to wince and continued cooking as if nothing had happened. Each time I remember this I laugh, but I learned my lesson and hope to never make that same mistake again. Another funny thing happened while I was taking some bananas out of the oven. I accidentally set the oven at a higher temperature than needed, and when I pulled them out, they looked like charcoal! We all laughed it off on the show because—whether you're on live TV or at home in your own kitchen—that's what cooking is all about: having fun and enjoying yourself. So each time you make a mistake, keep in mind that (1) it could be worse—you could be on live TV; and (2) the great advantage of cooking is that you can always start over!

In this section, we will explore everything you need to know to achieve fantastic flavors. We'll start by learning the most common mistakes that even experienced chefs make. Then I'll guide you through basic knife skills, cooking techniques, and shopping strategies. This entire journey will help you spend less time in the kitchen without skimping on flavor and quality.

most common kitchen mistakes

The best way to conquer your fear of cooking is to accept that it's okay to make mistakes. We all make them, and that's how we learn! Having said that, I do want to help you make the fewest possible mistakes so you don't have to waste time remaking dishes. That's why I've prepared a list of the most common kitchen mistakes. I've put this together based on my own personal experience as a chef and a restaurant patron, and even from my own home and TV mishaps.

- **Not reading the entire recipe:** A recipe shouldn't be the end all and be all; however, it's especially important for beginners to pay attention to the recipe instructions to make sure not to skip a crucial step, which could ultimately result in having to make the dish again or having to eat an unappealing meal. For this reason, I've made my recipes simple, easy to follow, and flexible enough that you can add your own personal touch if desired. In fact, tweaking recipes is a surefire way to develop your own cooking style and discover the combinations you and your family like most.

- **Not trying the dishes:** Believe it or not, one of the most common mistakes among home cooks is not tasting what they make before putting it on the table. This is equivalent to buying a car without test-driving it first. How will you know if your dish tastes good unless you try it first? You simply must try the food while preparing it. I recommend you do this in several stages so you have the chance to adjust the flavors according to your taste. At my restaurant, I tell my cooks that they must try absolutely everything: not all tomatoes taste the same, not all soups taste the same, even after they've been made, and food flavors change with each passing day. You must constantly try *everything* while you cook!

- **Not measuring ingredients:** In the interest of speed, many times we measure ingredients by eyeballing, meaning we estimate ingredient amounts rather than using the appropriate tools to ensure accuracy. This is fine if you already have some kitchen experience. However, if you're a novice, I recommend that you follow the recipe measurements, especially if you're baking, since a mistake in this case could mean your cake won't rise or your muffins will have an undesirable texture. Sacrificing accuracy for speed is also responsible for dishes lacking in vibrant flavors. Even worse, if you're preparing food for a group, by not measuring the ingredients, you might leave someone without a serving. This would be a tragedy.

■ **Using low-quality products:** When it comes to choosing ingredients, never has the saying "you get what you pay for" been more accurate. It's worth spending a little more money to get high-quality ingredients. The quality must be there in the ingredients in order to make a good dish. If you feel an ingredient is not good enough, it's best not to use it so that you don't spoil your recipe. You'd be surprised how many times I see an aesthetically appealing dish only to try it and realize that the ingredients used were not at their best, and so the quality of the recipe is diminished. I recommend that you not rush when choosing ingredients, so that when it's time to cook them, they are at their best and you don't have to waste time on several trips to the supermarket. Remember that as soon as a vegetable is separated from its plant, it begins to deteriorate and lose freshness and nutritional properties; the fresher it is, the better.

> The great advantage of cooking is that you can always start over!

■ **Cooking all your food over high heat:** Whether it's lack of time or lack of patience, many people tend to cook all their food over high heat, thinking that the higher the heat, the quicker the cooking time. However, cooking over high heat is a technique to be used only when required, such as when searing cuts of meat, vegetables, or fruits. Cooking all foods over high heat could backfire. For example, high heat is good for cooking the outer parts of food but not the middle. If you always use high heat, the outside of the food will be cooked but the inside will not be. High heat also increases the chance that food will stick to the pan. So pay attention to the recipe and use the levels of heat it recommends.

■ **Frying several ingredients at once:** It's easy to be tempted to fill the deep fryer with ingredients, thinking that this saves time. However, this actually makes the food take longer to fry, and you even risk some pieces

remaining partially or completely uncooked. You also might find that you aren't getting the desired crunchy texture. Some time ago, while working at a banquet, I was short on time and decided to fill the deep fryer to the rim while making fried calamari. This lowered the oil's temperature, and the cooked calamari did not have the correct texture. I recommend you fry food in small quantities. This will give each piece the proper amount of space and time to cook—and you will make better use of the oil and the deep fryer.

■ **Over- or under-salting:** Another common cooking mistake is not adding the right amount of salt to a dish. This is a crucial point because salt is incredibly important when flavoring food. Salt is used not simply to make food less bland. It's used to enhance or strengthen a recipe's flavor; that's why it's included in baking and dessert recipes. The best way to prevent mistakes with salt is to add it in small quantities, so you can adjust it while you cook. It's much easier to fix a dish lacking in salt than to fix one with too much salt, although there are ways to save an excessively salted dish. For example, add pieces of raw, unpeeled potato to oversalted stews, sauces, and soups. As it cooks, the potato will absorb the excess salt. Remove the potatoes before serving the dish. If you add too much salt to vegetables, simply place them under running water, then reheat before serving. For oversalted dressings or vinaigrettes, try adding a dash of oregano. To help control how much salt you add to a recipe, add it from above, placing your hand at head height. This helps distribute the salt evenly over the food and helps you avoid under- and oversalting.

■ **Overcooking:** You did everything right while preparing the recipe and now your dish is cooking. You feel good; you know that soon you'll be enjoying a delicious meal. Suddenly, your phone rings, you lose track of time, and you forget to turn the heat off, and now the food is overcooked. Avoid this colossal mistake by simply paying a little more attention to time. We use timers that ring at the restaurants, but you could use your cell phone, since all smartphones nowadays have timers and alarms. Make use of this gadget to remind you when to take food off the heat. It will save you lots of time and disappointment down the road.

■ **Not washing your hands:** Before you handle food, you should make sure your hands are clean. I always emphasize this point at my restaurant because hands harbor many germs that can easily transfer to food and ultimately affect the health of those who eat it. Just like a surgeon washes his hands before operating on a patient, you must also do so before cooking.

- **Not washing food before eating it:** Just like our hands, we must thoroughly wash all food to make sure it's clean before cooking. Remember that many ingredients travel long distances and are handled by many people before reaching the supermarket. All this handling means food carries germs and pesticides that you do not want as added ingredients in your dishes. Wash food right before using rather than before storing; washing before storing can shorten the life of many vegetables.

how to chop ingredients like a star

Knives are a chef's best friend. There's nothing more relaxing to me than the sound of a knife chopping away on a cutting board. As a child, I liked watching my mom chop and listening to the different sounds each food made. There's something about the constant movement and repetition that makes this activity relaxing and therapeutic.

While we must respect the knives in our kitchens, we mustn't be afraid to use them. With some practice, you'll get better and faster at chopping and slicing ingredients, just like a professional chef. Make sure you work at a speed that's comfortable for you. It's best to take a little longer today and chop faster later, rather than cutting yourself today and losing your love for cooking.

There is a great variety of kitchen cuts, including the julienne, *bâtonnet* (cut into batons or sticks), paysanne (diced), fermiere (country-style), *rondelle* (round), cubed, crosswise, and oblique. Beginners don't need to know them all but it's good to familiarize yourself with the terminology.

The first thing is get used to cutting all ingredients on a cutting board. Occasionally, if you're short on time, you may be tempted to chop on any flat kitchen surface, and even I admit to doing this. However, this can damage the knife and subsequently make you lose more time when chopping in the future, or even worse, it could scratch your kitchen counter. To avoid this, always have a clean cutting board within reach.

Before cutting any ingredient, you should wash it and make sure you're getting rid of any impurities. Then let it dry (you can wrap it in a paper towel to accelerate the process).

This step is especially important when you're working with herbs, because if you chop them wet, they may turn into a kind of puree, which would spoil your efforts.

To chop effectively and safely, always cut the food in half or slice it so that it has a flat surface you can turn down while chopping; it will be stable and safer to cut. And of course, no one wants to waste precious time searching for an onion that rolled from the cutting board to the floor underneath the dining table.

It's important to shape the hand you use to hold the ingredient like a claw. Remember to hide your nails and let the side of the knife slip against your knuckles when cutting. This will let you control the knife and will make you feel safer.

Although some of you may already know this, it's important to remember that the knife you use should be the right one for the food you are chopping. Avoid chopping small ingredients with large knives. This will only slow you down.

Another important point when chopping is always to keep your eye on what you are cutting. This will help you make same-size cuts, which is key so that they are a uniform size for cooking. It's simple: If you want to chop like a star, you must pay close attention to what you're doing. Avoid distractions such as your phone or the TV while chopping. I always say that the sum of small details carried out successfully achieves perfection.

cook with less fat without sacrificing flavor

Eating well is not just about enjoying rich, succulent dishes; it's also about nurturing ourselves. And being a good home cook does not only mean making delicious food; it also means being conscious of unnecessary fat and calories that go into what we and our families eat. It is possible to make wholesome and nutritious meals without sacrificing flavor. There are many easy ways to reduce calories from our recipes. Best of all, you can do it without anyone noticing.

I admit that at home, my family wasn't always healthy when it came to eating. My parents are Arab, and their rich lineage and culture have to some extent shaped the way I cook and combine flavors. And although Arab food is generally very healthy, we loved eating the most fattening dishes at home.

During my childhood, starting my day off with falafel was normal. Then I'd have baked kibbe for lunch with lots of butter, prepared by my mother, who still makes it deliciously well, and dinner started with some fried eggplant followed by a sandwich with shredded meat—classic Armenian cooking. It wasn't a very balanced diet at all, and the problem isn't eating these types of dishes every so often, but rather making them part of your regular diet.

Because of these habits, I was overweight at the start of my teenage years, which affected many aspects of my life, such as sports, the clothes I wore, and my behavior with friends. Although my food choices were a major catalyst, my passion for food was what ultimately inspired me to do some research on how to eat better and maintain a healthy body. I learned to like and appreciate food for its great variety of flavors, textures, and aromas, and this curiosity led me to follow my calling in the culinary world.

When I began my education, I quickly discovered that there are many ways to cook healthy dishes that are satisfying and full of flavor. On a personal level, this newfound skill proved invaluable for reaching my ideal weight. As a result, I was fit enough to take up sports such as tennis and karate and be at my best for games and competitions. As I learned more about cooking, making balanced meals at home felt effortless. Soon I managed to change my family's eating habits, and they were none the wiser! You can do the same at home by following these key points:

- Trim meat of its visible fat. With a sharp knife, carefully separate the lean meat from the fat. If you're eating chicken or turkey, make sure to remove the skin before cooking.

- Season your food with fresh spices. Spices are low in calories yet loaded with flavor. No one will miss the fat if a chicken breast or piece of meat is well seasoned.

- To brown chicken, meat, or fish with fewer calories, season with olive oil, salt, and pepper in a deep dish before cooking. After seasoning, move just

As a child, I liked watching my mom chop and listening to the different sounds each food made.

the food to the pan, letting the excess oil remain in the dish. It's a simple technique that will help you keep the scale where you want it.

- Use healthier thickening agents. Thickening agents are ingredients added to increase a food's density without affecting the flavor. Some are starch based, such as flour, and others are protein based, such as egg yolk. Thickening agents can be very important, for example, in sauces, stews, and purees, and if they're used correctly, they considerably improve the food's presentation and texture. They can really help give your dishes that wow factor. However, some thickeners, such as beurre manié (flour with butter) and heavy cream, can add too many calories. For sauces, stews, and soups, a good alternative to butter is cornstarch. It has much less fat than butter, which lets you cut calories, and it does a good job as a thickener. Another healthier choice for a thickener is blended oats instead of flour. Oats have more fiber and protein than flour, which will help satisfy your hunger for a longer period of time.

- Grill, steam, or bake rather than frying food. A roasted chicken or an oven-baked fish can be as delicious as the fried version. In fact, most food tastes better when grilled, seared, or broiled—basically any cooking method that involves a high source of heat that usually browns the top or edges of the food. The only thing to keep in mind is not to use excessively high heat since you risk overcooking the outer parts of the food while leaving the inside uncooked.

different cooking methods

Cooking, beyond following a recipe, is an art and a philosophy. And like all art, cooking can be done in many ways. The more risks you take, the more confidence you'll have to create amazing dishes. Now, when I talk about different cooking methods, I mean the different techniques used to cook food. Let's explore this further.

- **Pressure cooking:** If you're the type to cook enough for two or three straight days, this method was made for you. Pressure cooking allows you to prepare large quantities of food quickly, healthily, and effectively. As my mother says, it's worth mentioning the obvious in this case: The first thing you need in your kitchen is a pressure cooker. This useful tool makes the boiling point increase to above 212°F by causing the pressure inside it to rise to higher than atmospheric pressure. Food cooks faster because of the high pressure and temperature.

Given its power, a pressure cooker is ideal for cooking grains, vegetables, and fibrous and fatty meats. I find it particularly interesting because it allows you to turn a tough, cheap cut of meat into an amazing dish! The high temperatures loosen the meat's fibers and make the fat melt, which gives the entire pot a delicious taste. As if that weren't enough, it usually cuts the cooking time by half, as shown below:

Fibrous meat cut + Vegetables + Regular pot: 3 hours
Fibrous meat cut + Vegetables + Pressure cooker:
   1½ hours

With that said, you must keep certain things in mind when using a pressure cooker. The first is time: A few extra minutes at these extreme temperatures could mean the difference between a dish with amazing flavor and one that's not so appealing. It all depends on the time the recipe calls for.

Additionally, each time you use the pressure cooker, remember that you must fill it to only two-thirds of its capacity. It's also important to place the cooker on a burner that's the same size as or smaller than the base of the cooker. And if you're going to stew vegetables, fill the cooker only halfway, as vegetables tend to swell during cooking and may obstruct the release of steam. If you want to save energy and money, lower the heat when the cooker has reached its highest level. This will not affect your food, but your pocket sure will notice it when you get the gas and electricity bills.

■ **Grilling:** This technique is ideal for people who are in a constant rush, like me! It's ideal for cooking red and white meat given its speed and convenience. A metal griddle or grill is used above a source of constant heat, such as charcoal, fire, or an electric burner. This cooking method requires very little preparation, given that you must only spread some oil on the food so that it doesn't stick to the surface. Besides being fast, it's one of the healthiest ways to cook since grilling doesn't add any extra calories, compared to frying. You can add flavor by marinating the meat with whatever you like, such as salt, pepper, or aromatic herbs. And if you're really short on time, cut the protein lengthwise into thin strips so that they cook faster.

I always say that the sum of small details carried out successfully achieves perfection.

Additionally, by slicing the protein into thin strips, you're also helping to brown them, which will add a delicious texture to your dishes.

- **Slow cooking:** In contrast to the pressure cooker, the slow cooker is designed to cook food at very low temperatures over long periods of time, usually between 4 and 12 hours. These electric cookers have a mechanism that traps heat, which allows them to control the temperature.

  The slow cooker is ideal for stews, sauces, and even meats. The best part of this pot is that it can save you work in the kitchen, given that you hardly have to prep the food before cooking it. It's just a question of adding the ingredients to the cooker—chopped if they're vegetables—and voilà!

  This tool is extremely popular in the United States because you can basically set it up and forget about it. Food cooks at low temperatures, between about 158°F and 194°F, which means you don't have to keep checking the water level, because the water does not evaporate. Many people turn the slow cooker on before leaving for work, then come back home, turn the cooker off, and enjoy a delicious meal. If you do this, place the slow cooker in a clear, open space on the counter, as you would with any device that emits heat.

  Another advantage of slow cooking is that a portion of the meat gelatinizes and becomes part of the stew's liquid, which guarantees a stronger flavor. Since the cooking time is longer than in conventional cooking, this tool does wonders with meat's texture. You can easily turn a cheap cut of meat into an exquisite, world-class dish. Just remember that for this method, patience is key!

- **Steaming:** In my opinion, steaming is one of the most fascinating cooking methods! Just as it implies, steaming consists of cooking food with steam generated by boiling liquid. To carry out this method easily and quickly, there are special two-part pots, with a bottom part to hold the boiling liquid and a top part that has holes to let the steam flow through to cook the food. Pay close attention to avoid overcooking, and don't allow the food to come in contact with the boiling water below, so as not to affect its texture. No one likes watery vegetables or meat (unless they're in a soup).

  One of the things I like most about steaming is that it's extremely healthy and, when done well, delicate meats, such as fish, will be flaky and tender and melt in your mouth. With this cooking method, you add flavor with sauces and vinaigrettes, since there's no need to add anything to the food while cooking it.

A subtler way to flavor steamed food is to season the cooking liquid with spices and aromatic herbs. The flavors are infused into the steam, which comes in contact with and delicately seasons the food. For example, I usually make a steamed fish with white wine as the cooking liquid, to give the dish extra flavor. After the fish is cooked, I reduce the wine (boil off the extra liquid to concentrate the flavor) and use it as a sauce to make a delicious low-calorie meal. Steaming also preserves a food's vitamins and nutrients, allowing you to make highly nutritious meals. For all these reasons, it's commonly used among dieters and in weight-loss plans.

> # Cooking, beyond following a recipe, is an art and a philosophy.

■ **Frying:** The most delicious culinary vice is fried foods. Although it can add a lot of calories, when used in moderation, frying achieves a crunchy texture that we all love. It's also one of the easiest and quickest cooking methods around. Here are some useful tips to avoid common, time-consuming mistakes.

First, there are two ways of frying food: You can immerse it completely in oil, also known as deep-frying, or you can cook it in a pan using anything from a shallow layer to very small amounts of fat, also known as pan-frying. The style you use will depend on the recipe, but it's more common to pan-fry food.

What follows is an explanation of deep-frying. Before you start, I recommend that you get a cooking thermometer. Cooking temperature is key, and a thermometer lets you verify the oil's temperature at all times so that you can cook safely and optimally. The ideal temperature for deep-frying is 375°F. If the oil isn't sufficiently hot, the food will absorb more fat than it should, resulting in a less-than-satisfying texture. It's recommended that you use oils with sufficient heat tolerance, such as corn oil, canola oil, or coconut oil, the latter being the healthiest of the three.

When deep-frying, make sure the food is cut into sizable pieces so that it cooks properly. If the food is too large or thick, you run the risk of undercooking even if the outer part is golden and crispy. By the same token, if the food is too small or thin, you can just as easily overcook it. One thing

you'll notice when deep-frying food is the bubbling of the oil, which is caused by water evaporating from the food, quickly drying it. This is what allows us to achieve that delicious crunchy texture. If you are looking to add world-class quality, a tried-and-true way is to observe the color. A deep-fried ingredient that is exceptional should always look opaque, never shiny. If it's shiny, the food likely absorbed too much oil and will not have that light and subtle texture found in dishes at high-end restaurants. But don't give up if you don't get it right the first time. Simply check the oil's temperature and start over.

If you're watching your calorie count, I recommend you do what I always do at home. After deep-frying, I drain excess oil by placing the food on a couple of folded sheets of paper towel. This doesn't mean the food will turn into a low-calorie dish, but the paper does absorb some of the oil, thus reducing some of the fat.

- **Baking:** The oven is the kitchen device that will give you the most satisfaction as a chef. There are basically two very different ways of using it: roasting and cooking au gratin. For roasting, you'll use the oven for a long period of time at about 375°F. This slow cooking will reward you with an amazing flavor that cannot be obtained with any other method. The oven's dry heat helps seal meat quickly, trapping its juices inside. The result is a true utopia for the mouth, the meat browned on the outside and juicy in the inside. Typically, the oven is used for big cuts of meat, such as ribs, lamb shanks, whole turkeys, and so on. It's best to start the cooking process with an adequate temperature to seal the meat, usually 400°F, later lowering it to make sure the inside cooks well too. When roasting food, dedicate enough time to avoid common mistakes due to lack of time. While you can put food in a slow cooker and forget about it for hours, when it comes to the oven it's best to keep an eye on it.

    The au gratin method is enti rely different because it cooks food fast at a high temperature. What we want in this case is to form a golden layer on top of the food, usually by cooking butter, cheese, bread crumbs, and sauce at a high temperature. The usual temperature for au gratin is between 400°F and 500°F. As you would with the pressure cooker and roasting, pay close attention to the time so you don't overcook or, worse, burn your dish.

    When done well, cooking au gratin is an interesting skill that will delight any home cook since the food's texture is so delicious that you can use it to negotiate favors with your family and get them to do some extra house-hold chores. My mom always made pasta au gratin when she wanted us to help her with chores around the house!

- **Poaching:** This delicate cooking method takes some time and patience, but it is definitely worth learning. It consists of slowly cooking food by immersing it in liquid that's below its boiling point. I say liquid because it doesn't necessarily have to be only water; you can also use liquids aromatized with herbs and spices, wine, fruit juices, or a combination. They all add flavor to the poached food.

    The foods that best lend themselves to this cooking method are fish, such as salmon and grouper, any type of poultry, and finely cut meat. It's also a great method to make egg dishes, such as the classic and delicious eggs Benedict. Poaching eggs gives them a delicate texture. Additionally, it gives the eggs a signature look that enhances the dish's presentation. This is one of my preferred cooking methods for eggs.

    To poach food, you must choose a pot large enough to completely immerse the ingredients in the poaching liquid.

    The liquid's temperature is the key to poaching, and to make sure that you're doing it right, I recommend that you use a cooking thermometer, keeping the liquid between 176°F and 185°F. To poach entire pieces of fish, chicken, or meat, the cooking process must begin while the liquid is still cold; it is heated to poaching temperature while the food is already immersed in it. If the meat is already cut into pieces, the liquid

should be at the desired temperature before the meat is immersed for poaching.

Each food has a different cooking time, but red meat tends to take the longest. In general, calculate 1 hour of cooking for every 2 pounds. For fish, allow 15 minutes for every 2 pounds. When it comes to fruits and vegetables, ideally cook them between 8 and 10 minutes. Finally, eggs can be cooked in just 4 minutes, which makes them a great ingredient for practicing your poaching skills.

If you're careful and you use a thermometer, you'll be poaching food like a pro in no time!

how to shop like a chef

Extraordinary food depends a lot on the freshness and quality of the ingredients you use. They play an incredibly important role in the preparation of any recipe. You can't expect to end up with a delicious dish when the ingredients aren't optimal. It's like constructing a building with defective blocks; it simply will not prosper.

If possible, always choose fresh fruits and vegetables over frozen or canned ones. Fresh food tends to have a purer taste than frozen or canned. However, there will be times when, due to time constraints, you'll need to turn to canned or frozen food. That's fine, as long as you use them in moderation.

Fortunately, nowadays, in most supermarkets it is easier than ever to find incredible, high-quality ingredients. You just need to know where and how to look for them. The following are my personal tips for choosing better ingredients so that the opportunity to cook results in a delicious and satisfying meal.

how to choose fresh fruits and vegetables

Knowing how to choose fresh produce will save you untold amounts of time! I've always thought that eating fresh vegetables and fruits is the key to being healthy. A growing number of articles mention the positive effects clean veggies and fruits have on our bodies and minds. I've read fascinating stories of people who treat illnesses with just fresh fruits and vegetables. These superfoods contain vitamins and minerals that help the body in astonishing ways.

When choosing fresh vegetables or fruits, there are several things to consider. First, check to make sure the fruit or vegetable is firm enough. Lightly squeeze it to see if it's soft to the touch. If it's too soft, it's safe to assume it's past its shelf life; however, if it's too firm, it needs more time to ripen.

This brings us to the second factor: ripening time. Some fruits and vegetables, such as plantains and mangoes, become overripe quickly; therefore, if you aren't going to use them within a few days, it's best to buy them "green," or not quite ripe yet.

Another important factor is color. As I always say in my shows, you must use all your senses when it comes to cooking, so carefully observe the color of your ingredients when buying them. Inspect them to see if they've been bruised or mistreated. If it's possible to taste a fruit or vegetable before you buy it, this is best, but by no means am I suggesting that you take a bite out of an apple to see if it's ripe enough and then leave it on the shelf. Some supermarkets will let you sample their produce. If that's the case, take advantage of this offer and visit more stores that offer free samples since it will save you a lot of time and money in the long run.

Smell is also very important. When these ingredients are perfectly ripe, you'll be able to appreciate their aroma through their skin or peel. This is especially the case with fruits since they tend to be more aromatic than vegetables, so don't forget to use your sense of smell.

It's especially important to pay attention when choosing green vegetables. It can be tricky to choose the best from the bunch, but it doesn't have to be difficult if you know what to look for. My rule is as follows: The greener they look, the fresher they are. If you are still in doubt about a specific vegetable, ask a supermarket employee to make sure you're choosing excellent-quality ingredients.

seasonal fruits and vegetables

Although nowadays we can get a great variety of fruits and vegetables in any super-market regardless of the season, it's worth knowing a bit about seasonal freshness. Don't worry, I'm not going to make you study all of the world's plants by season! Seasonal foods vary by climate, country, and altitude; at the very least, you should be aware of the seasonal fruits and vegetables that grow in the region where you live. Not only is choosing seasonal whole foods economically and environmentally smart, but it also has health advantages.

> You can't expect to end up with a delicious dish when the ingredients aren't optimal.

In fact, there is a correlation between seasonal health and seasonal foods. Nature offers us plants that optimally grow in a particular season and that also help our bodies fight off weather-related illnesses. For example, vitamin C is vital during the months of winter, and that's why in places that experience cold weather, fruits such as oranges, tangerines, and kiwis are in season. The high dose of vitamin C in these plants helps the body fight off the common cold and flu, which are most viral during the winter. In the summer, when we need to protect our skin from the sun's rays and stay hydrated, some of the fruits and vegetables available are watermelons, melons, and cucumbers. They all have very high levels of water and beta-carotenes, which are essential skin protectors. This natural phenomenon helps us understand why certain fruits and vegetables thrive during certain seasons and conditions while others don't.

When you find a fruit or vegetable in the market that is not in season, it's because it was grown under unnatural conditions with the help of chemical substances to reach ripeness, or it has traveled long distances to reach your supermarket. Both reasons directly affect the nutritional value of the fruit or vegetable, which is why you and your family will benefit more from seasonal ingredients. Moreover, the transportation costs to deliver these ingredients hike up not only the prices but also carbon emissions.

Another reason to buy seasonal ingredients is that they are more flavorful because they're fresh and harvested when ripe, which is crucial if you want your dishes to be extraordinary! Also, when you buy seasonal fruits and vegetables, you can try foods you normally wouldn't buy because of the price tag. When in season, these ingredients will not be as expensive as they are out of season, since they are produced in mass quantities, and if in the end you don't like them, at least you didn't spend a fortune. I love this point because it urges you to try something new that might inspire you to create a fantastic recipe at home.

Buying seasonal ingredients also helps support farmers' markets. I truly enjoy buying from local farmers because it's a good way of making sure that the products are fresh. And as a plus, the people are always very friendly and willing to share some of their own cooking tips.

Use the Internet to educate yourself on the different fruit and vegetable calendars of the region where you live. Check these calendars when planning your weekly menu, to find out which ingredients are in season.

Also, supermarkets often point out which fruits and vegetables are in season because they're also interested in selling them quickly. If you're still in doubt, don't be afraid to ask an employee; they're trained to know what ingredients are in season. So next time you go food shopping, make sure to buy some seasonal ingredients. They're the start to a delicious recipe!

buying organic fruits and vegetables

During the last few years, the organic movement has grown immensely popular. Its mission is to raise awareness about the unnatural conditions under which food, namely plants, is grown and produced and how this directly affects our health and the environment, paving the way for the distribution of organic foods.

For those who are not familiar with the facts, organic fruits and vegetables that are sold in markets and by local farmers were not treated with fertilizers or pesticides in the soil where they were grown or during any of their production stages. Basically, by eating organic you are eating 100 percent natural food, which means you're consuming 100 percent nutritious food with virtually no traces of chemicals or pesticides that could affect your health and well-being in the long run.

A crucial and sometimes crippling issue when buying organic is the price. Producing organic fruit and vegetables is expensive because producers and farmers do not have the assistance that comes with using chemicals; therefore, the growing process is slower. Fertile soil that uses only organic fertilizers needs to rest more than other types before the next crop. This means production is lower, and the lower the supply, the higher the product price.

But this doesn't mean organic produce isn't within everyone's reach. It just means we need to be smarter when it comes to buying organic. Find your local farmers' markets, which should be searchable online. Prices in these local markets are better than prices in the big chain stores because they take out the middleman and you're buying straight from the source.

Another tip to help you stay within your budget is to choose organic fruits and vegetables that are truly worth the price and effort. For instance, I pay special attention to the produce listed as the most toxic by the U.S. Department of Agriculture. By choosing only organically grown versions of these fruits and vegetables, you're making sure you're not consuming chemicals that are harmful to your health. The list of the most toxic conventionally grown produce includes:

- celery
- peaches
- strawberries
- blueberries
- apples
- peppers
- spinach
- cherries
- kale
- potatoes
- grapes

The reason these plants are more prone to retaining pesticides and chemicals is because they easily absorb water, which means they also easily absorb pesticides. I recommend that you invest a little more money and buy organic when it comes to these fruits and veggies.

I also want to share with you the list of fruits and vegetables that you don't have to buy organic, which will help save you money. None of these foods easily absorb pesticides. These include:

- onions
- avocados
- yellow corn
- pineapples
- mangoes
- peas
- kiwi

- cabbage
- eggplant
- melons
- watermelons
- asparagus

As you can see, you have several options for buying healthy produce without breaking the bank. However, if you want to buy everything organic, and at a good price, consider becoming your own organic producer. Regardless of whether you live in a house or an apartment, whether big or small, you can grow and enjoy your favorite whole foods right at home. Chiles are one of my go-to ingredients and ones I use often, so I decided to stop buying them at the supermarket and start growing them myself. I now have

It's worth knowing a bit about seasonal freshness.

fifteen varieties in my garden. With a little time and patience, anyone can plant their own vegetables, and the Internet is filled with information on the type of equipment you need and the steps to take to ensure a fruitful harvest. Also, most plants don't need round-the-clock care; so long as you water them a couple of times a day, you will have done enough for them to thrive. Best of all, you can save a lot of money once you start growing your own organic produce at home!

how to choose fresh meat and fish

Primal cuts of meat and fish tend to take the lead role in main dishes. Carnivores like me know that they are the difference between a good meal and a boring one. What's more, some countries are internationally renowned for having the best meat. Argentina is well-known for the quality of its beef, Peru for its fish and seafood, and Spain for its ham. You, too, could be recognized by your friends and family for how well you prepare different primal cuts. To start, just like with plants, you need to understand and choose the right cuts of meat.

- **Beef:** To choose fresh red meat, use your senses of sight, smell, and touch. A piece of fresh meat must be vibrant red throughout. If there's any discoloration, it means the meat wasn't handled or refrigerated well. Also look for blood residue, and try to buy meat that doesn't have much. By the same token, look at the color of the fat. It should be white and creamy, not yellowish. Above all, the meat shouldn't smell acrid or rancid.

We need to be
smarter when it
comes to buying
organic products.

Make sure to buy in established stores, in other words, places that you know through word of mouth or the Internet that traditionally sell good, fresh meat. These are the places I trust the most because I can establish a relationship with the butcher, which in turn allows me to get better deals and cuts. Check the sell-by and expiration dates, since refrigerated meat stays fresh for just a day, and frozen meat for three weeks to four months. This is the only way you'll know if the meat is in good condition.

If you're looking for meat that will be quick to cook, look for cuts that are great for grilling. These cuts can be cooked immediately and don't require long amounts of cooking time. When the meat is cooked, slice against the grain to make the fibers shorter, rendering the meat tender and softer and easier to chew.

- **Poultry:** Just like with beef, it's best if you buy your cuts in established stores, from your trusted butcher. The first thing you will notice when choosing poultry is the skin's color. It should be white or light yellow and moist, without any discoloration or stains, and, critically, it shouldn't be sticky since a sticky texture indicates that the meat is about to expire, if it hasn't already. When you are buying chicken breasts, a key point to remember is that there shouldn't be too much fat between the meat and the skin.

  If you're buying packaged cuts, again, check the sell-by and expiration dates. Also, a good way to verify if the turkey or chicken is fresh is by looking at the edges of its wings. If the edges are somewhat darker than the rest of the wing, then the piece is not fresh. As with red meat, avoid chicken and poultry with lots of blood residue.

  If you're looking for the best cuts for grilling or to cook quickly, get the chicken breasts and thighs. These cuts, especially the thighs, are juicy and meaty.

- **Fish:** When it comes to choosing fresh whole fish, the first thing to check is the eyes. They must be transparent and bright. If you notice any dullness, the fish is not fresh. If the fish has already been filleted and you can't see its eyes, there are ways to determine its freshness. First, it should smell like the sea. A strong fishy smell usually means it's been lying around. The fillet should look moist and bright, as if it has just been cut from a fish caught right out of the water. If you can hold or touch it, gently press it with your fingers to see whether it quickly bounces back to its original shape. If it remains dented, it's not fresh.

Avoid buying all your fish for the week in just one day. If you're already taking the time to buy fresh fish, make sure to eat it that same day or at most within thirty-six hours of purchasing it. Don't refrigerate it to cook later, as it will lose its freshness and, with it, its quality. Keep in mind that whitefish is the easiest to use since its flavor isn't too strong. This means it combines well and complements other flavors, giving you a better chance to make an exceptional dish.

- **Pork:** The pig is the animal we get the most out of because we can prepare delicious dishes with almost all of its parts. Again, the meat's color will tell you how fresh it is and whether it's been mistreated. Make sure it has a light pink color, never brown. And just like beef fat, pork fat must look creamy and firm. Don't buy pork with thick skin or hair.

- **Lamb:** The younger and fresher the lamb, the less marinade it needs, since lamb is known for being tender and flavorful. The smell of fresh lamb is subtle and its color rosy. The fat should be white and firm. Lamb is usually prepared by roasting it in the oven. Calculate 15 minutes for every pound.

buying organic meat and wild fish

Just as you can with fruits and vegetables, you can also separate organic from mass-produced meats. In this case, the meat is organic when the animal did not consume growth hormones or antibiotics while it was raised and therefore doesn't carry any harmful substances that could pose a danger to our health.

Regarding meat, the subject of organic can be quite lengthy. Here is some vital information that will make you feel more confident when choosing organic meats and fish. Also, as a chef, I want you to know more about the ingredients we handle.

Let's start by talking about organic beef. Nowadays, there are two types of beef that can be certified as organic. The first is made up of cows that have been grass-fed

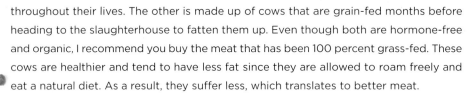

throughout their lives. The other is made up of cows that are grain-fed months before heading to the slaughterhouse to fatten them up. Even though both are hormone-free and organic, I recommend you buy the meat that has been 100 percent grass-fed. These cows are healthier and tend to have less fat since they are allowed to roam freely and eat a natural diet. As a result, they suffer less, which translates to better meat.

When it comes to poultry, such as chicken and turkey, buying organic is also important. The need to speed up their growth is aided by increasing the amount of hormones and antibiotics in the feed. It's crucial to look at the label when buying poultry and make sure it's certified organic. Be mindful of labels such as "pastured," which are meant to make you believe the chicken is more natural, when in fact, this label doesn't guarantee that the poultry is hormone- and antibiotic-free.

The same goes for pork. When pigs are raised organically, their diet consists of organic food, and they have access to grass, wild apples, and acorns, versus the conventionally raised pig, which has a permanent diet of corn and soybeans. The organically raised pig also enjoys more land, space, and light during its life, which makes for healthier and better-quality meat for us.

With regard to lamb, we can apply the same organic principle—hormone- and antibiotic-free. When buying this type of meat, keep in mind that the season when lamb is most tender is during the early summer or May and June. You can usually find both local lamb and lamb imported from New Zealand, both of which are available in organic versions.

When it comes to fish and seafood, there is no label in the United States that certifies organic. It's not possible to determine what the fish is eating, regardless of whether it's wild or farm raised, which is why it cannot be called organic. What's more, even though farm-raised fish diets are controlled, they still come in contact with seawater, which is polluted with toxic substances. Therefore, farm-raised fish cannot be called organic either. Instead, fish are divided into two categories: wild caught and farm raised.

As the name implies, wild-caught fish are those that are trapped in their natural habitat. They tend to be healthier than farm-raised fish because they don't have to share a small space with many other fish or suffer the illnesses that this type of environment can cause. For this reason, I recommend you buy wild-caught fish. But be warned. Any type of fish has some level of mercury, a toxic element present in both wild-caught and farm-raised fish. Usually, bigger and older fish such as swordfish and shark have the highest mercury levels, so it's best to avoid consuming large quantities of these fish. Stick to buying fish such as hake, sardines, and catfish, and seafood such as shrimp, crab, and squid, because of their low mercury levels. Whenever possible, buy local fish and seafood because they tend to be fresher.

As when you buy organic produce, avoid spending too much money for organic meat and poultry and wild fish by buying directly from the producer. Also, anytime you can, buy large quantities and freeze what you aren't using that same day. The exception is fish and seafood since you want to use it the same day you buy it. Buying from the producer also allows you to negotiate the price and get better deals. Another thing you can do to stay within your budget is be a smart consumer. Sacrifice things like sodas, chips, and snacks that aren't healthy for you and invest the money in organic and wild products. These foods are better for you and, in the long run, more cost-effective, especially when you aren't racking up health and medical bills to manage a food-related illness.

Sacrifice things like sodas, chips, and snacks that aren't healthy for you and invest the money in organic and wild products.

. . . the organic movement has grown immensely popular. Its mission is to raise awareness about the unnatural conditions under which food, namely plants, is grown . . .

shortcuts and other useful cooking tricks

The one thing I wanted to be sure to include in this book is the list of fun and ingenious shortcuts and tricks that will make cooking easy, pleasant, and efficient. This list has everything, from how to open difficult jars to how to chop faster. A little ingenuity goes a long way in the kitchen.

how to easily open jars

As a guy, I've dealt with the suffering and shame of not being able to open a jar of food. This usually always happens during family gatherings, and naturally, all my cousins tease me about it. One Sunday, I was expecting my whole family over for dinner. I'm talking about my entire family: aunts, uncles, countless cousins—a big crowd. I had set out some snacks for people to munch on while I prepared the food and realized there were no more olives. When I tried to open a new jar, the lid would not budge. I quickly noticed a cousin staring at me from afar and knew he'd soon jump on this opportunity to start teasing me. After several jokes and laughter, I managed to open it. It can happen to anyone, but thankfully I've finally found a solution to end this embarrassing problem. Next time you have to open a jar, avoid letting your hands slip by using a tennis ball to grip the lid. All you have to do is cut the ball in half and use the inside to get a firmer grip. The rubber adheres to the jar lid, giving you the traction you need to open it.

how to quickly aerate wine

One of the best ways to improve the taste of red wine is through aeration. When wine comes into contact with air after spending some time bottled up, it loses the enclosed aromas and, with them, some of its acidity, which improves the wine's sensory effect, in that the aroma and flavor will be purer. Usually, at a restaurant, to aerate wine, a wine steward or server pours it through a decanter or Vinturi wine aerator, a gadget that aerates the wine as it is served. You can aerate wine at home if you have enough time, but even if you've organized a get-together at home and don't have a lot of spare time, don't worry because you can still aerate your wine. If you don't have a decanter or a Vinturi wine aerator, one way you can get this done is by pouring the bottle of wine into a large pitcher and then into another pitcher, then back into the first pitcher, and so on. You must do this about fifteen times to aerate the wine, and believe me, it will be of great help. After this process, your wine will have been aerated enough to serve. And that's how easily you can improve the taste of your wine in very little time.

how to perfectly peel a hard-boiled egg

One of the most exasperating tasks a home chef can endure is peeling a hard-boiled egg. For those who don't know how to do this, the process can be frustrating because the entire shell doesn't come off easily and many times you find yourself infuriated,

peeling tiny pieces of shell stuck to the outside of the egg. But here's a shortcut I learned: Next time you boil an egg, grab a thumbtack or a clean, pointy object and make a small incision in the thinnest part of the eggshell. Make sure to puncture the inside membrane as well as the shell. Then place the egg in boiling water, without the thumbtack, and let it cook. Once the egg is cooked, place it under cold water, and then, using a spoon, carefully crack open the hole you created and separate the shell from the egg. If you do this very carefully, you'll find that the shell comes off easily and the egg is cooked to perfection.

One of the best ways to improve the taste of red wine is through aeration.

how to make sure ice cream is always ready to serve

If you eat ice cream, you've probably noticed that once you open it and put it back in the freezer, it tends to lose that initial creaminess. There's nothing worse than bending a spoon when you're trying to scoop cementlike ice cream, then wasting time waiting for the ice cream to thaw a bit before serving. Fortunately, there is a solution to make sure ice cream remains as creamy as the first time you tried it. All you need is an airtight Ziploc bag. Just place the ice cream container in the bag before you return it to the freezer. And if you forget to put it in a Ziploc bag, you can always put the ice cream in the microwave for a few seconds to soften it up.

how to simultaneously cut small ingredients

You don't need to have the skill of a hibachi chef to cut small ingredients at lightning-fast speed. With this shortcut, you'll be able to cut several small ingredients such as cherry tomatoes, olives, and berries in a jiffy and, more important, without losing a finger. To do this, find any two same-size plastic lids. They can come from containers, powdered milk cans, whatever you want. Place the ingredients to be cut between the two lids, essentially making a sandwich. Apply pressure to the top lid so you can hold the ingredients in place while you slide the knife between the plastic lids and through the ingredients. In this way, you will have cut several ingredients quickly and safely. Get ready to break the speed-cutting record at home!

how to cut with dental floss

As I mentioned, knives are your best allies in the kitchen; however, there's one unusual item that doesn't even belong in the kitchen that will come in handy: dental floss. You can use this personal hygiene tool to cut through soft food surfaces and, best of all, you won't have to waste time washing it afterward. It's exceptional for cutting cakes, peeled bananas, cheeses, and even cooked potatoes. You'll find it very handy because it allows you to chop almost effortlessly, reducing the chances of making a mess and helping you obtain precisely cut pieces. Be sure to buy unflavored dental floss—without the minty flavor!

how to separate the egg yolk from the white (without making a mess)

Some recipes instruct you to separate the egg white from the yolk, and if you've never done it before, it can be somewhat complicated. One of the most popular ways to do this is to break the egg and hold it over a bowl as you transfer its contents between the two halves of the shell until all the white falls into the bowl and only the yolk remains in the shell. However, if you're in a rush, this might not be the best option. Fortunately, there's a very simple trick that can be used in any kitchen. You just need an empty plastic bottle, preferably a water bottle. First crack all the eggs you're going to use into a deep dish. When you're done—this is where the magic begins—grab the uncapped plastic bottle and squeeze it gently to push a little of the air out of it. Place the bottle's mouth over one of the yolks you'd like to remove and stop squeezing the bottle. The bottle will expand to refill with air, and in this suction process, it will remove the yolk from the white. Place the yolk in a separate dish and repeat the process. You will soon be enjoying a great dish with eggs full of protein! And if, like me, you enjoy making the most of an ingredient, you can store the yolks and make your own mayonnaise.

how to make your cake last longer

Cakes are delicious, but they're always best when eaten fresh. With time, they lose their spongy and soft texture, more so when they've already been sliced—and no one likes that! Thankfully, there's a way to solve this problem with something most of us have at home: slices of bread. The trick lies in covering the cut parts of the cake with slices of bread. You can use toothpicks to keep them in place. As the days go by, you'll see that the outer layer of bread will keep the cake moist and in perfect condition.

how to make the most of a jar of spreadable chocolate

No matter how much we try not to leave the least bit of chocolate stuck to the jar, we always leave some behind. It's practically impossible to get it all out! But in this world, there is a solution to everything, and with this simple and delicious trick you'll be able to get every last drop. Next time a jar of chocolate is nearly finished, pour 1 cup of hot milk into the jar and stir. The hot liquid will melt the spread, making delicious instant chocolate milk. Transfer into a cup and you're all set to enjoy this treat.

how to get rid of the strong smell of fish when cooking

The only bad thing about cooking a delicious piece of fish at home is the unpleasant smell it releases when it comes into contact with heat. This is particularly annoying inside a home with few windows and limited access to fresh air. We all know what happens: The smell lingers in the house no matter what air freshener you use. But don't fear! Here's a tip to avoid this nuisance: Soak the fish in milk for at least an hour before cooking it. This will help enhance the fish's flavor and leave your house odorless.

As you can see, the kitchen is a place where creativity never dies. There's always an ingenious and fun way of carrying out the activities that every chef must do to make amazing dishes. And with these ten simple tricks, I guarantee that your experience in the kitchen will greatly improve.

The kitchen is a place
where creativity
never dies.

let's get to work!

the capital of the culinary world is in latin america

Before diving into the delicious recipes in this book, I want to share with you what inspired me to write several of them. There has always been talk about European and Eastern cuisine as excellent references within the culinary world. We've all tried, in some shape or form, the delicacies that come from French, Italian, Chinese, and Japanese cuisine; however, the different culinary styles of Latin America are slowly but surely making a name for themselves in the culinary world. And since I'm a chef with Hispanic influences, this unprecedented event has inspired me to represent it with all my might.

Thanks to my profession, I've had the amazing opportunity to visit a lot of Latin American countries and to experiment with many different dishes and delicacies. Through these experiences, I've witnessed the wonderful creative mix of ingredients used in the cuisines of these diverse countries. Latin America has such a wide variety of foods and ingredients, even more than other places, and this abundance has helped us create new and delicious world-renowned dishes.

Through the recipes in this book, I want to share a piece of that creativity and good flavor. My hope is that they inspire you to cook more often, even every day if at all possible. I've traveled to the faraway corners of Mexico, Peru, Ecuador, Argentina, Chile, and Honduras, to name a few, always very alert, absorbing every culinary experience so that you can enjoy it on your table. However, this doesn't mean I haven't also included the classic Mediterranean recipes that were a big part of my upbringing. Simply put, I am just proud to celebrate the wonderful moment Latin American cuisine is experiencing.

So without further ado, it's time to put into action everything I've shared with you and make the kitchen a place where you can create unique flavors that will delight your loved ones on a daily basis. It's time to become a great chef at home. Let's get to work!

perfect appetizers

It's food's debut, the table's first dish, which creates anticipation and excitement for the grandeur that awaits! An appetizer has the powerful ability to set the tone for the entire meal. Once, on a very busy night at one of my restaurants, we had an altercation with a customer because it took us a little longer than usual to seat him. Understandably, the client was upset and his behavior toward our waiters was less than favorable. I knew I had to do something to make this gentleman happy, to spare him from spending a bitter evening simply because he'd had too long a wait. So I ran to the kitchen and prepared bacon-wrapped dates and fried cassava with a delicious chimichurri sauce, and I sent the two complimentary appetizers to his table. The result was just what I expected! The client calmed down immediately and ended up leaving a generous tip as well as doing something that has always been very important to me: He gave the restaurant a great review online. This is a true story that proves the power of a good appetizer.

Likewise, a bland appetizer can ruin a meal. A poor experience with this first dish can leave your guests or loved ones thinking that the rest of the meal will follow the same pattern. I have eaten countless times at restaurants that don't pay much attention to this, and the truth is, it can be quite unpleasant. However, with these recipes, you can rest assured that your appetizers will always be spectacular.

I've included a wide variety of appetizers: There are those I call "from the garden," made with raw or cooked vegetables and fruits; those whose main ingredients are made of wheat and flour, such as bruschetta, crackers, and sandwiches; and those with protein. The general rule is that the flavor of these appetizers should never overshadow that of the main course. Also, it is customary to begin with lighter dishes and progressively move on to heavier ones, or to begin by serving the cold dishes, followed by the hot dishes.

Personally, when it comes to appetizers, I like mixing textures and flavors to make my guests' meals a great culinary experience. I try to combine classic appetizers to encourage people to try new ones, such as the delicious Caesar Soup with Chicken (see page 103), which, let it be noted, works magically on the palate. Having said that, I don't like spending too much time in the kitchen preparing appetizers because the idea is to share them with guests, and I know you're thinking the same at home. That is why I included a great variety of appetizer recipes that won't take up too much of your time and will allow you to impress even the most demanding of palates. And, as always, you can expect all of them to carry that wow factor that makes all the difference.

fried calamari with marinara sauce

SERVES 4

This is a popular dish that I serve at my restaurant, Sabores by Chef James, but instead of marinara sauce, it comes with a coconut sauce, which is unexpected. However, as delicious as the coconut sauce is, making it is rather labor intensive. The last thing I want to do is make your life difficult, so for the purpose of convenience, I've opted to include a marinara sauce, which is the classic and crowd-pleasing dip for calamari. The secret to great calamari is to cook it for a very short time, since overcooking will turn calamari hard and rubbery. This is a perfect recipe to share with guests!

INGREDIENTS:

canola oil

2 cups flour

2 tablespoons smoked paprika

1 tablespoon black pepper

salt

1 pound calamari rings

2 lemons for garnish

FOR THE TOMATO SAUCE

½ yellow onion

2 cloves garlic, peeled

2 carrots

2 stalks celery

olive oil

32 ounces crushed tomatoes

½ cup basil, chopped

4 bay leaves

CALAMARI PREPARATION:

1. In a large pot, preheat the canola oil to 375°F.

2. In a shallow bowl, mix the flour, paprika, black pepper, and salt.

3. Place the calamari rings in the flour mixture to coat.

4. Put the coated rings in the hot oil and fry for about 1½ minutes. Remove the calamari with a slotted spoon and place on a plate lined with paper towels.

SAUCE PREPARATION:

1. Mix all the vegetables except the crushed tomatoes in a food processor for 1 minute or until vegetables are finely chopped. If the food processor cannot take large amounts, do this in batches.

2. In a large pot, add a drizzle of olive oil and sauté the vegetable mixture over medium heat for about 7 minutes.

3. Add the crushed tomatoes, basil, and bay leaves.

4. Cook for another 40 minutes over medium heat.

5. Place some sauce in a small bowl.

6. Serve the calamari in a plate with the sauce on the side

chef james tip >> Use a kitchen thermometer to make sure the oil is at 375°F before adding the calamari. This will make the temperature drop to 350°F when you place the calamari in the oil, allowing for a perfect fry.

poblano chile quesadillas

SERVES 4

This dish will transport you to beautiful and beloved Mexico. When heated, Oaxaca cheese becomes very elastic, making this recipe a unique culinary experience. You can easily find this cheese at any grocery store. During the time I spent in Los Angeles, I would drop by next door to my uncle's barbershop almost every day to eat enchiladas and poblano chile quesadillas. They are delicious! Simple, quick, and cheap, this is everything we look for in a convenient recipe.

INGREDIENTS:

> 2 poblano chiles, cut into strips and seeded
>
> 1 red onion
>
> salt
>
> pepper
>
> 4 (10-inch) flour tortillas
>
> 1 pound Oaxaca cheese or queso fresco

PREPARATION:

1. Add the poblano chiles, onion, salt, and pepper to a pan over high heat and sauté quickly, until the onion softens and is slightly golden, about 3 minutes. Remove from the heat.

2. In a large pan (or over a grill pan), warm each tortilla over medium heat and add some cheese on the top half of the tortilla. Once the cheese has melted, sprinkle each tortilla with a quarter of the onion–poblano chile mixture, and fold the tortilla in half.

3. Flip the quesadilla and cook for 2 more minutes.

4. Cut in quarters and serve.

5. Repeat steps 2 through 4 for each tortilla.

> ## chef james tip >>
> If you roast the poblanos over high heat in the oven or over an open flame, you will obtain an incredible smoky flavor that will give these quesadillas a whole new dimension.

octopus a la gallega (galician octopus)

SERVES 4 TO 6

This recipe brings back such fond memories of Galicia, renowned for having the best-quality shellfish in Spain. I began eating this dish when I was five or six years old while visiting my neighbor, Mr. David, who later inspired me to become a chef. We would get an early start and buy fresh octopus, and he would go back home to cook it. His trick was to cook it with a cork in the pot, since that's how they made it in his native Galicia, generation after generation. There was never a logical explanation for why the cork helped the octopus stay soft but, truth be told, it was always very tender.

INGREDIENTS:

 1 clove garlic

 1 whole potato

 1½ pounds octopus

 ¼ cup olive oil

 salt

 smoked paprika

PREPARATION:

1. Fill three quarters of a deep pot with water. Add the garlic, potato, and octopus. Cook over medium heat until the potato is cooked, about 40 minutes. The octopus will cook at the same time. Don't allow the water to boil; otherwise the octopus hardens.

2. Once cooked, cut the potatoes in cubes and arrange them on a plate to serve as the base of the dish. Then place the octopus on top of the potatoes.

3. Let it cool down a little and serve with the olive oil, salt, and smoked paprika sprinkled over the top.

chef james tip >> To get the cooking time exactly right, calculate about 9 to 10 minutes per pound of octopus. Also, if the water where you live has high levels of calcium and chlorine, add an unpeeled onion to the pot before you begin cooking to absorb these impurities, or use filtered water.

avocado soup with shrimp

SERVES 4

This recipe was one of the first cold soups I made. I once had a cold strawberry soup on a cruise and I found it so interesting that it led me to search for more cold soup recipes. Gazpacho was at the top of my list, but later I discovered an avocado soup that I felt was unparalleled; still, I felt something was missing. That is why I added the shrimp and other touches of my own inspiration. If you haven't tried a cold soup, here's your chance. It's excellent during the hot summer months.

INGREDIENTS:

3 Hass avocados, pitted

1 cup vegetable broth

2 tablespoons green onions, chopped

2 tablespoons cilantro leaves

2 tablespoons lemon juice

salt

white pepper

¼ cup heavy cream

3 tablespoons olive oil

kernels from 2 ears of corn

1 teaspoon smoked paprika

4 jumbo shrimp

PREPARATION:

1. Place the avocados, vegetable broth, green onions, cilantro leaves, lemon juice, salt and pepper in a food processor and process for 1 minute.

2. Add the heavy cream, mix to blend, and set aside.

3. Combine the olive oil and the corn in a pan and sauté over high heat until the corn begins to caramelize.

4. Add the smoked paprika and the shrimp and continue to sauté for 3 more minutes.

5. Pour the cold soup into four individual bowls and garnish with the sautéed shrimp and corn.

green gazpacho

SERVES 2 TO 4

Even though I had already tried gazpacho, given its diverse preparations outside Spain, I wanted to try the authentic Andalusian gazpacho on one of my trips to the Iberian Peninsula. This dish is characterized by its simplicity, tradition, and culture. A fun fact about gazpacho is that it is considered to be a mix between soup and salad because of its ingredients. Also, gazpacho comes in different colors, from red (if you use tomatoes) to green. In this case, I decided to create a variation of a green gazpacho based on the original recipe, so you can prepare it at home whenever you feel like it.

INGREDIENTS:

- ⅛ cup sherry vinegar
- ½ cup olive oil
- 1 cup vegetable broth
- 1 clove garlic
- 1 shallot
- 2 cucumbers, plus more, cubed, for garnish
- 1 cup green grapes, plus more, cubed, for garnish
- 1 teaspoon dill, chopped, plus more for garnish

PREPARATION:

1. Combine the vinegar, oil, broth, garlic, shallot, cucumbers, grapes, and chopped dill in a blender and blend for 3 minutes.

2. Pour the gazpacho into individual bowls and garnish with the cubed cucumber and grape and chopped dill.

lentil soup with chorizo

SERVES 6

Lentils, lentils, lentils! My mother loves them with a passion, but as a kid, I hated them. Because they are inexpensive and because they can feed many, my mother prepared lentils frequently when we had just arrived in the United States and when money was scarce. She used to prepare a huge pot that lasted for 3 or 4 days . . . 4 days of torture for me! It was not until I started my cooking courses that I began to grow fond of lentils. I saw that people really liked them, and when you're a chef, you don't cook for yourself! When I make them, I like to infuse them with flavor and take advantage of their creamy texture. So I present to you the recipe that made me a believer in lentils.

INGREDIENTS:

2 chorizos, sliced

olive oil

½ cup carrot, chopped

½ cup celery, chopped

½ cup onion, chopped

½ cup leek, chopped

2 cloves garlic

1 teaspoon cumin

2 tablespoons red wine vinegar

2 tablespoons tomato paste

1 pound lentils

8 cups chicken broth

PREPARATION:

1. In a deep pot, over medium heat, cook the chorizo with a little bit of olive oil to release its flavor. Add the vegetables, garlic, and cumin and sauté until vegetables become soft.

2. When the vegetables start to turn golden, about 5 to 7 minutes, add the vinegar, tomato paste, and lentils and cook over medium heat until the lentils are lightly toasted, about 1 minute.

3. Add the broth and allow the soup to cook over low heat for 1 hour.

4. Serve in a bowl.

chef james tip >> Double the quantity of all ingredients so you'll have leftovers. It's a smart way to save time in the kitchen!

traditional guacamole

SERVES 6

To me, one of the most fascinating Mexican foods is guacamole. As part of its name (*mole*) indicates, it's a sauce, which I find extremely versatile; it goes with everything. Not to mention it's super easy to make and a crowd-pleaser. Where there's guacamole, there are happy people! Or that's my case, at least. Every time I offer my friends a *molcajete* filled with guacamole, the reaction is always a happy one. Try it at home and let me know how it goes through social media.

INGREDIENTS:

    2 Hass avocados
    salt
    ½ red onion, chopped
    1 jalapeño, chopped
    juice of 1 lemon
    2 tablespoons cilantro, chopped
    corn tortillas

PREPARATION:

1. In a big bowl, mash the avocados with a fork. Season with salt and add the rest of the ingredients.

2. Keep mixing until all the ingredients are evenly combined.

3. Serve with the corn tortillas.

chef james tip >>
To prevent the guacamole from turning dark, you can add half a teaspoon of lemon salt, a citric acid that helps prevent the avocado's oxidation. You can find this product in Mediterranean markets.

guacamole with grilled pineapple

SERVES 6

When I opened my first restaurant, Sabores by Chef James, I wanted to create a guacamole bar with different touches and textures, but without sacrificing the speed and
ease so characteristic of the classic recipe. After a good meeting with my chefs, we
added an original touch: grilled pineapple. It was a hit at my restaurant, and it will
surely be a hit in your home.

INGREDIENTS:

2 Hass avocados

½ red onion, chopped

1 jalapeño, chopped

juice of 1 lemon

2 tablespoons cilantro, chopped

4 tablespoons grilled pineapple (see chef james tip below), chopped

corn tortillas

PREPARATION:

1. In a big bowl, mash the avocados with the back of a fork. Season with salt and add
the rest of the ingredients.

2. Keep mixing until all the ingredients are evenly combined.

3. Serve with the corn tortillas.

chef james tip >> To make the pineapple spectacular, grill it over
very high heat. Don't panic when it's time to flip it; usually 5 minutes on
each side will yield the perfect marks.

carrot and curry soup

SERVES 4 TO 6

Carrot soup is definitely one of those recipes that make you feel good. Creamy and hot, it's fantastic, which is why my mother and aunts prepared it so often. I wanted to modify the recipe to end up with a carrot soup with more character, so I added a series of ingredients from Thai cuisine. The best thing is that, as with any other soup, you can prepare it very quickly. Once you try this version, you will experience a uniquely incredible taste.

INGREDIENTS:

    2 tablespoons coconut oil
    1 teaspoon red peppercorns
    1 onion, chopped
    1 tablespoon ginger, peeled and chopped
    1 tablespoon curry powder
    6 carrots, roughly chopped
    3 cups vegetable broth
    16 ounces coconut milk
    cilantro

PREPARATION:

1. In a large pot, combine the coconut oil, peppercorns, onion, and ginger, and sauté over medium heat until the onions become translucent. Add the curry powder and cook for 2 minutes.

2. Add the carrots and cook over medium-high heat for about 5 minutes, stirring constantly. Once the carrots are soft, pour in the broth and let the soup cook for about 10 minutes over medium-high heat.

3. Add the coconut milk and let the soup cook for 10 more minutes to allow the flavors to blend. Serve garnished with cilantro.

chef james tip >> Make sure you cook the curry and oil well. Otherwise, you will be left with the sharp flavor of raw curry.

pepper and cauliflower cream

SERVES 4

This soup will make even people who don't like cauliflower ask for a second serving. The pepper gives it a vibrant orange color and a touch of sweet and roasted flavor; bacon provides a smoky profile. Just writing about this recipe makes me drool.

INGREDIENTS:

4 cups whole milk

2 cups cauliflower, chopped

3 strips bacon, chopped to ½-inch pieces

2 cloves garlic, peeled and chopped

1 red pepper, roasted and chopped

2 bay leaves

1 teaspoon cumin

1 teaspoon coriander

1 potato, peeled and cubed

1½ cups vegetable broth

green onions, chopped, for garnish

PREPARATION:

1. Combine the milk and cauliflower in a large pot and cook over low heat for 20 minutes.

2. In a different pot, cook the bacon over medium-high heat until crispy. Transfer the bacon bits to a plate, leaving the fat in the pot.

3. In that same pot, add the chopped garlic, followed by the pepper, bay leaves, cumin, coriander, and potato.

4. Add the cauliflower-milk mixture and the broth. Cook for another 10 minutes, and blend with a handheld immersion blender.

5. Pour the soup into individual bowls and garnish with the chopped bacon and green onions.

ecuadorian ceviche

SERVES 4

This recipe reminds me of beaches in several Latin American countries, where you can always find fishermen selling ceviche made on the spot, served in small plastic glasses. The ceviche that stands out in my mind is the Ecuadorian ceviche. I was intrigued that it was prepared with tomato sauce and mustard, which is contrary to the style of the typical Peruvian ceviche. It's delicious and ideal to prepare midweek, when you're short on time.

INGREDIENTS:

1 pound shrimp, tails removed

2 tomatoes, chopped

½ serrano chile

juice of ½ orange

juice of ½ lemon

2 tablespoons tomato juice

2 tablespoons ketchup

1 tablespoon cilantro, chopped

1 tablespoon honey

2 tablespoons olive oil

¼ red onion, chopped

green onions, chopped, for garnish

PREPARATION:

1. Mix all the ingredients except for the green onions in a bowl and put it in the fridge. Let it sit for about 5 minutes to chill the ceviche.

2. Garnish with green onions and serve.

chef james tip >>
I recommend serving this ceviche with fried bananas, also known as *mariquitas*.

nikkei ceviche

SERVES 2

Thanks to the significant migration of the Japanese to Peru, the world was introduced to *Nikkei* cuisine, a fusion of Peruvian and Japanese ingredients and preparations. This ceviche is a great dish if you are trying this fascinating, exotic, and unique cuisine for the first time.

INGREDIENTS:

3 ounces tuna, cubed

salt

⅛ teaspoon yellow chile pepper paste

2 limes

⅛ teaspoon ginger, minced

⅛ teaspoon garlic, minced

¼ teaspoon simple syrup

⅛ teaspoon rice vinegar

½ teaspoon celery cream (blended celery)

2 tablespoons soy sauce

½ teaspoon toasted sesame oil

1 teaspoon cilantro, chopped

nori (seaweed to roll sushi), cut into thin strips

½ teaspoon sesame seeds

PREPARATION:

Place the tuna in a bowl and season with salt. Add the chile pepper and mix. Repeat this step for the rest of the ingredients, making sure to add the cilantro, *nori* strips, and sesame seeds at the end.

chef james tip >>
You can find *nori* at any Asian market. This ingredient adds a complex and very characteristic flavor to my version of this ceviche.

aguachile

I learned this recipe at the Mayan Riviera in Mexico. It was an incredible experience since I was taken to a village where the natives didn't speak Spanish, and even then we still managed to communicate perfectly. This taught me that food is a universal language that we can all speak. Aguachile is very similar to ceviche but with a style all its own. It has a delicious flavor because it carries the spice of habanero chiles, which complements the fish so well.

INGREDIENTS:

1 red onion, chopped into large cubes, plus more for garnish

1 cucumber, chopped into large cubes

8 tablespoons cilantro, chopped

4 habanero chiles, chopped

1 teaspoon salt

juice of 10 lemons

1 pound whitefish, chopped

2 Hass avocados, cubed

3 radishes, chopped

PREPARATION:

1. In a cocktail shaker, combine the onion, cucumber, cilantro, and chiles, followed by the salt. Shake to dehydrate the vegetables.

2. Add the lemon juice to the mixture, shake, and set aside.

3. In a deep plate, combine the fish, avocado, extra chopped onions, and radishes.

4. Add the liquid mixture from the cocktail shaker and let the dish stand for 2 minutes before serving.

chef james tip >> Make sure you cut the fish cubes evenly so that they all take about the same time to marinate and "cook" in the lemon juice. This way you will avoid having some pieces that are more raw than others.

tiradito

This is another Peruvian delicacy that I couldn't leave out of this book. It's very similar to ceviche, since it tends to follow the same principle. But what sets tiradito apart is the delicate fine cut, or thin slicing, of the fish. The presentation is spectacular and fast and will make you look and feel like a star chef.

INGREDIENTS:

1 pound tiradito or whitefish, thinly sliced

4 yellow chile peppers, finely chopped

¾ cup lemon juice (about 6 lemons)

1 clove garlic, minced

¼ cup olive oil

salt

1 ají limo chile pepper

2 sweet potatoes, boiled

PREPARATION:

1. Place the fish slices on a plate.

2. In a blender, combine the yellow chile peppers, lemon juice, garlic, and olive oil, and blend for 1 minute. Season the sauce with salt and pour the sauce over the fish.

3. Sprinkle with chopped ají limo to taste, and serve with the boiled sweet potatoes.

peruvian ceviche

SERVES 4 TO 6

I was very fortunate to try ceviche long before Peruvian cuisine started expanding around the world. A good friend of mine from Peru who worked with me years ago introduced me to it, and I had wanted to travel to Peru to try it ever since. When I finally had the chance to go, I used the trip to perfect recipes, learning from those who really knew about ceviche. As the result of all that passion and effort, I created this version of the traditional Peruvian ceviche, which I hope you will enjoy.

INGREDIENTS:

- 1 pound whitefish
- salt
- 2 tablespoons yellow chile pepper paste
- ½ red onion, chopped
- ¼ cup cilantro, chopped
- juice of 8 lemons

PREPARATION:

Mix the fish with the salt and chile, followed by the rest of ingredients. Keep mixing for 2 minutes. Serve in a chilled individual bowl.

chipotle hummus

SERVES 8 TO 10

If there's one thing that I always have in my refrigerator at home, it's hummus. Because my family is Arab, we always made it at home. We would have it for breakfast, dinner, and sometimes even an afternoon snack. To this day, I still make it. This classic recipe is one from my childhood, but I give it a twist by using chipotle chile, which adds another dimension of flavor. No doubt, this will be better than any hummus you can get at the grocery store.

INGREDIENTS:

>   2 15-ounce cans garbanzo beans
>   ¼ cup water
>   ½ cup tahini
>   2 chipotle chiles
>   2 cloves garlic
>   1 teaspoon cumin
>   lemon juice
>   salt
>   pita bread
>   olive oil

PREPARATION:

1. Mix all the ingredients, except the pita bread, in a blender for 2 minutes. Season with salt.

2. Brush the pita bread with olive oil, and toast it on both sides in a pan over medium-high heat.

3. Serve the hummus in a bowl with the pita bread on the side.

> **chef james tip >>** If you use canned garbanzo beans, make sure you wash them thoroughly before using to eliminate excess sodium.

yuquitas with jalapeño chimichurri

SERVES 6 TO 8

These *yuquitas* are the perfect and easy way to entertain your guests at a get-together at home. Served with *chimichurri* sauce, these crunchy treats can be addicting. Take it from me: You eat one and you just can't stop. I decided to use cassava (another name for yuca) in this recipe because it's a wonderful starchy food that doesn't get the recognition it deserves, compared to, say, the potato. For this recipe, fried cassava is far superior to fried potatoes. I just hope you potato lovers don't get too upset with me.

INGREDIENTS:

1 cup oil, for frying

2 cups cassava, cut for fries (½ inch thick)

FOR THE *CHIMICHURRI*

1 cup cilantro

1 cup parsley

2 jalapeños, charred on a pan

3 cloves garlic

¼ cup red wine vinegar

1 cup olive oil

¼ teaspoon cumin

PREPARATION:

1. Heat the oil to 375°F (use a kitchen thermometer).

2. Add the cassava and fry until golden.

3. While the cassava is frying, combine all the *chimichurri* ingredients in a food processor and mix for 1 minute.

4. Serve the cassava fries with the *chimichurri* on the side.

chef james tip >> For a texture closer to the original *chimichurri*, try not to process the ingredients too much when preparing them.

beef *anticuchos*

This is a great appetizer that will make your gathering with family and friends start off on the right foot. I will never forget the day I tried it for the first time. I was invited to the house of some Peruvian friends and they said we were going to eat *anticuchos*. This was before I began my culinary studies and I had no idea what they were talking about. After doing some investigating, I learned that *anticuchos* were a type of grilled marinated kebab, and of course, I happily accepted their invitation. After I had eaten about fifteen *anticuchos*, we were told that the *anticuchos* were made with animal heart. Since I had eaten heart many times before, I didn't mind, but everyone else's reaction was the opposite. For this recipe, I use beef tenderloin so that everyone can enjoy it, no problem. Putting together this delicious dish will take you less than an hour, and you will leave everyone wanting more.

INGREDIENTS:

1 pound beef tenderloin, cut into 1-inch cubes

15 bamboo skewers

cilantro, chopped, for garnish

FOR THE *ANTICUCHERO* MARINADE

½ cup ají panca chile pepper

⅛ cup white vinegar

½ teaspoon oregano

1 clove garlic, minced

1 teaspoon cumin

2 ounces soy sauce

4 ounces hoisin sauce

PREPARATION:

1. Pierce the beef cubes with the bamboo skewers and set aside.

2. In a blender, combine the marinade ingredients and blend for 1 minute.

3. Place the kebabs in a container or tray and add the marinade. Let the meat marinate for 30 minutes.

4. Place the kebabs on the grill over high heat. Cook for about 2 minutes on each side and serve garnished with chopped cilantro.

melted cheese with chorizo

SERVES 2

In Latin America we call it "melted cheese"; in Europe they call it "fondue." Originally, this dish was created to bring families together and encourage people to sit around a table to eat with others, a tradition that was slowly dying in Switzerland, the dish's country of origin. We, of course, adapted it and gave it its own personality using chorizo, and we eat it with tortilla chips. One cold beer, please, with my melted cheese!

INGREDIENTS:

- 1 Mexican chorizo, thinly chopped
- ¼ onion
- 2 cloves garlic, minced
- 1 tomato, chopped
- 1 cup shredded Monterey Jack or Oaxaca cheese
- 6 6-inch flour tortillas, warm

PREPARATION:

1. Cook the chorizo in a cast-iron pan over medium-high heat for 3 minutes.

2. Add the onion and garlic and cook for 2 to 3 minutes.

3. Add the tomato and cook until almost all the liquid has evaporated.

4. Remove the chorizo mixture from the pan and add the cheese to the pan. When the cheese melts, add the chorizo mixture on top. Serve with the tortillas.

tortilla soup

SERVES 6 TO 8

This is one of the most flavorful soups in Mexican cuisine and yet another great example of how a combination of different textures elevates the diner's experience of the dish. You will love the crunchy bite of tortilla with the soup's creaminess. Simply put, this is a delicacy for all of us who appreciate the universal language of food.

INGREDIENTS:

8 cups chicken broth

olive oil

2 pasilla chiles, veins and seeds removed

2 ancho chiles, veins and seeds removed

5 tomatoes, chopped

5 cloves garlic, minced

¾ yellow onion, chopped

salt

pepper

5 corn tortillas, cut into ½-inch strips

½ cup Cotija cheese, crumbled

1 Hass avocado, cubed

cilantro

lemon

PREPARATION:

1. Pour the chicken broth into a large pot over high heat and bring to a boil. Allow to simmer over low heat.

2. In a frying pan over medium-high heat, add oil, and lightly toast the chiles. Mix the chiles in a food processor with the tomatoes, garlic, and onion. Strain immediately by running the mixture through a colander to get rid of lumps.

3. Put the mixture in the pot with the chicken broth, season with salt and pepper, and allow to cook for about 20 minutes to blend the flavors.

4. Separately, fry the tortillas until they are crunchy. Set aside.

5. To finish, serve the soup with the tortillas, cheese, avocado, and cilantro. Add a splash of lemon to taste.

shrimp *al ajillo* (garlic shrimp)

SERVES 2

This is one of the best ways to cook and serve shrimp as an appetizer. Even better, it's nutritious and ideal for those who are watching what they eat. On a personal note, this recipe brings back many memories of my childhood, when I visited my neighbor and first mentor, Mr. David, on weekends. Recalling his particular recipe with my palate's memory alone, I present it here for you.

INGREDIENTS:

olive oil

4 cloves garlic, chopped

⅛ teaspoon red peppercorns

8 jumbo shrimp, peeled

2 tablespoons brandy or sherry

1 teaspoon Italian parsley, chopped

1 cup cooked white rice

PREPARATION:

1. In a pan over medium-high heat, pour a drizzle of olive oil over medium-high heat. Add the garlic to the pan and sauté until the garlic is lightly brown.

2. Add the red peppercorns and shrimp and sauté until the shrimp turns pink.

3. Add the brandy and let the alcohol evaporate for about 2 minutes. It should display a syrupy consistency.

4. Add the Italian parsley to taste and serve with the white rice.

chef james tip >> If you use large shrimp with heads, save the heads. Once the dish is prepared, squeeze the juice from the shrimp heads into the flavored oil that you used to cook the shrimp to make a sauce with spectacular flavor.

squash and ancho chile soup

SERVES 4

You can enjoy this delicious soup in under 45 minutes. This dish is ideal for cold days, although it tastes so good that you will want to eat it whatever the weather. The spicy-sweet touch of the ancho chile gives great richness to the squash flavor. I used my mother's traditional squash soup recipe but added a dash of ancho chile for the soup's distinct flavor.

INGREDIENTS:

- 2 pounds squash
- 2 tablespoons olive oil
- 1 onion, chopped
- 2 tablespoons basil, chopped
- 1 tablespoon mint, chopped, plus more for garnish
- 1 tablespoon ancho chile powder
- 8 black peppercorns
- 2 cinnamon sticks
- 12 coriander seeds
- 4 cups chicken broth
- 2 tablespoons heavy cream
- mint, for garnish

PREPARATION:

1. Preheat the oven to 375°F and roast the squash until you can pierce it easily with a knife.

2. Meanwhile, in a soup pot over medium heat, pour in the olive oil and sauté the onion, basil, 1 tablespoon of the mint, chile powder, peppercorns, cinnamon sticks, and coriander until the vegetables start to sweat. This should take about 3 to 4 minutes.

3. Cut up the roasted squash into small pieces and add it to the vegetable mix, followed by the broth.

4. Bring the soup to a boil over high heat. Reduce the heat and simmer on low for about 30 minutes. Add the heavy cream.

5. Blend with an immersion blender and serve, garnished with a touch of mint.

grilled corn with chipotle mayo and cotija cheese

SERVES 4

It's because of recipes like this one that I love cooking. This dish transforms simple ears of corn into a marvelous street snack. It's simple to make, using ingredients you can find almost anywhere. Serve as an appetizer or as a side dish when you're cooking on the grill.

INGREDIENTS:

4 ears corn, shucked

olive oil

salt

pepper

1 cup mayonnaise

juice of 1 lemon

3 chipotle chiles

2 tablespoons honey

1 cup shredded Cotija cheese

cilantro, chopped

PREPARATION:

1. Preheat the grill to high or preheat the oven to 400°F.

2. Season the corn with olive oil, salt, and pepper. Place the ears on the hot grill or in the broiler until they're charred, about 10 to 12 minutes.

3. Add the mayonnaise, lemon juice, chipotles, and honey to a blender and blend until smooth.

4. When the corn is ready, use a kitchen brush to spread each ear with chipotle mayonnaise.

5. Sprinkle with Cotija cheese and cilantro and serve.

caesar soup with chicken

SERVES 4

Let creativity take over your kitchen—we are going to transform the traditional Caesar salad into a delicious soup. You will be surprised at how good it tastes, and how lettuce, which is otherwise flavorless in the salad, gives it a fantastic touch. If you don't believe me, ask actress and television presenter Adamari López, who is a huge fan of this recipe, so much so that she took the time to ask me for the recipe before I published the book.

INGREDIENTS:

    2 tablespoons olive oil

    1 potato, chopped

    1 onion, chopped

    4 cloves garlic, chopped

    salt

    pepper

    3 cups chicken broth

    2 heads romaine lettuce, chopped

    ½ cup heavy cream

    ¼ cup whole milk

    2 chicken breasts, roasted and cubed

    ½ cup grated Parmesan cheese

    1 cup garlic croutons

PREPARATION:

1. In a large pot over medium-high heat, add the olive oil and sauté the potato, onion, and garlic for about 3 to 5 minutes. Season with salt and pepper.

2. Add the chicken broth and bring to a boil.

3. Add the chopped lettuce and allow it to cook for about 5 minutes.

4. Add the heavy cream and milk and cook for about 3 more minutes.

5. Blend the soup with an immersion blender and transfer to four individual bowls.

6. Garnish each dish with pieces of roasted chicken, Parmesan cheese, and croutons.

tortilla española (spanish omelet)

SERVES 6

This classic Spanish cuisine today finds a place on your table. You can serve it as an appetizer or even as breakfast, as my mother usually does. It is important to cut the potatoes uniformly—so that it's easier to eat—and to cook thoroughly over low heat to obtain the right texture: crunchy on the outside and creamy on the inside.

INGREDIENTS:

½ cup olive oil

1 pound potatoes, cubed

1½ yellow onions, finely chopped

6 eggs, beaten

PREPARATION:

1. In a pan over medium-high heat, add the oil, potatoes, and onions and fry until the onions are translucent.

2. Place the potatoes and onions in a colander and eliminate any excess oil.

3. Mix the potatoes and onions with the eggs and return to the pan. Cook over very low heat for 35 to 40 minutes.

my super nachos

SERVES 6 TO 8

This recipe gives original nachos a unique, fun identity. I found the inspiration in a nacho dish that I tried once at a restaurant with a couple of friends. I reconstructed it at home, applying my own touches until I created the version you're about to prepare. This is a great Sunday appetizer, especially if there's a game on!

INGREDIENTS:

- 1 andouille chorizo, chopped
- 1 onion, chopped
- 4 cloves garlic, minced
- 2 red chiles, chopped
- ½ pound ground beef
- 2 tablespoons tomato paste
- 1 cup chicken broth
- 1 15-ounce can red beans, drained and rinsed
- 1 bag tortilla chips
- mixed shredded Mexican cheese
- jalapeños, chopped
- sour cream
- cilantro, chopped

PREPARATION:

1. Sauté the chorizo in a pot over medium-high heat and remove.

2. In the same pot, sauté the onion, garlic, and chiles. Add the chorizo, ground beef, tomato paste, and chicken broth. Cook for about 40 minutes over medium heat, until the mixture thickens.

3. With 10 minutes to go, add the beans and remove the mixture from the heat.

4. Place the tortilla chips on a platter and cover with the beef and chorizo stew. Sprinkle with the cheese and jalapeños and top with the sour cream and cilantro.

perfect appetizers

a salad garden

We tend to see salads as diet dishes, bland and not adding much to meals other than nutritional value. Unfortunately, this reputation has pushed salads into secondary dishes that are commonly reduced to a sad combination of lettuce, tomatoes, and onions. It's no wonder that most restaurant salads go unnoticed by the culinary world. However, by the end of this chapter, and after trying these recipes, you will see salads as another opportunity to create incredible combinations of flavors and textures.

Because I was an overweight teenager, I devoted myself to searching for and improving flavors in salads. While trying to lose weight, I ate salad after salad every night and quickly got bored. It became my mission to find new salad recipes that I could make on a daily basis. I refused to accept that a dish in which one could combine so many ingredients, aromas, and textures should always look and taste the same. Once I got into the habit of loving these new salad mixes, I slowly began losing weight, and my take on salad has never been the same.

The secret to creating a good salad is to really understand what ingredients go well together to create unexpected and delicious combinations. The vinaigrette is also essential; this glorious liquid that dresses most salads plays a leading role, and it can be the difference between a super salad and a culinary catastrophe.

When it comes to salads, as with any dish, the quality of the ingredients is crucial. This is where you can benefit from a visit to a farmers' market. You can't beat the feeling of knowing that the meal on your table was harvested only a few hours before.

leading roles in a salad

A salad is much more than lettuce, tomatoes, and onions. There are endless ingredients you can combine, from different types of leaves, vegetables, and root vegetables to different kinds of meats and cheeses. That's why I've decided to expand on these ingredients a bit further before you venture into preparing these delicious recipes at home.

LEAF VARIETIES

Let me say right now that you must stop thinking of lettuce as the only option for a base in a salad. There are so many types of leaves you can find in any supermarket that the combinations are endless. In the following section, I share some of the many possibilities you can use as a base for your salad:

- **Lettuce:** Lettuce comes in many varieties, but the most common include romaine, iceberg, Boston, and Batavia. Romaine lettuce is usually used for the well-known Caesar salad due to its slightly bitter taste. Iceberg lettuce, shaped like cabbage, with crunchy leaves, is ideal for tacos and chicken *tinga*. Boston lettuce is ideal for Eastern or tropical salads. Batavia lettuce is available in a range of colors from brown to reddish and has curled leaves and a bitter taste.

- **Spinach:** Many enjoy using this amazing leaf as a base for salads. Uncooked spinach adds intense and brilliant color to salads. When it's fresh, its flavor and texture mix perfectly with raisins, pine nuts, walnuts, bits of toasted bacon, and Parmesan cheese. It's usually dressed with balsamic vinegars and sweeter dressings. Make sure you use it while it's fresh. Once spinach leaves start to wilt, the vegetable loses its distinctive flavor.

- **Arugula:** Arugula has become quite trendy, popping up on many restaurant menus. This leaf has a very particular taste, somewhat peppery. When you use it, make sure it doesn't overshadow the other condiments. It's usually combined with the same ingredients used with spinach.

- **Cabbage:** Out of all the leaves, this one undoubtedly adds a tougher texture and delightful crunch to a salad. Cut it into thin lengthwise strips so that it's easier to chew. Also, since it has a tough texture and is somewhat waterproof, it's best if you season it and let it sit for twenty minutes before serving to allow it to absorb the desired flavors. Cabbage goes amazingly well with carrots, celery, and cheese.

- **Endives:** Opaque white, green, and yellow, this leaf variety gives the classic green salad a different look. Its flavor is fresh and a little bitter, which makes it a great companion to blue cheeses, walnuts, caviar, and capers, among other ingredients.

PREPARING THE LEAVES

There are many leaves I haven't mentioned because they are less common, but there's a great variety. I invite you to try all the varieties you find in your farmers' market or supermarket, and soon you'll begin to discover new flavors and combinations. That's the beauty of cooking: You can always discover something new!

Now that you have a better understanding of salad bases, let's start preparing them. A very important first step is washing these leaves thoroughly. You never know what insecticide or chemical has been added to them; that's why I recommend that you always wash salad leaves, even if they come prepackaged and prewashed.

There are several ways to do this, depending on how many leaves you will be washing. First, make sure your kitchen sink is clean. Then fill it with water and add the leaves. Gently massage them in the water to remove any impurities.

Another method is similar to the above but on a smaller scale. Grab a container large enough to accommodate the number of leaves you plan on washing, and fill it with water. Drop the leaves inside and gently rub them. If you see a lot of dirt at the bottom of the container after doing this, change the water and repeat the procedure to make sure the leaves are clean. Once you've done this, dry the leaves well so that no water remains, as it could dilute the dressing. If you don't do this, you'll have a watery salad with a weak flavor.

To dry the leaves quickly, use a salad spinner or grab some paper towels and wrap the leaves in them. Gently pat to absorb every trace of water. If you notice the leaves are still wet, repeat the process with dry paper towels.

Now your leaves are ready for use. If you aren't going to use them immediately, you can store them in a sealed container and place them in the refrigerator. They will stay fresh up to four days. I recommend you prepare your salad greens over the weekend, when you can spare a little more time, so that when you want to use them during the week, they will be ready to go.

vegetables

Raw or cooked—whatever your taste buds desire!—vegetables can be part of a salad. Some of the most common vegetables used in salads are onion, corn, cucumber, olives, asparagus, and zucchini. If you're going to add them raw, I recommend that you peel and finely chop the vegetables so that they're not too difficult to chew and don't ruin your salad's texture.

Vegetables are a key component in a salad because aside from adding flavor, they influence the overall texture. Raw carrots can give an extra crunch to any salad, and crisp corn kernels can make it fresher.

I want you to get excited about salads because they're dishes in which creativity reigns and you can make your own rules regarding flavors and textures. With a good combination of vegetables, who knows what great salad you can come up with at home!

herbs

When used well, herbs can enhance the flavor of any dish and eliminate the need to use too much salt. However, because they're so flavorful, if you overuse them, they can overpower the dish's other flavors. The most common herbs you will use in vinaigrettes and dressings are basil, cilantro, parsley, rosemary, oregano, and mint.

You will see salads as another opportunity to create incredible flavors and textures.

cheeses

In a salad, cheese can be used as an ingredient or as part of the dressing. The usual cheeses used are Parmesan and blue cheese.

Parmesan cheese is a stellar ingredient in the classic Caesar salad. Its flavor and texture undoubtedly add a unique touch.

Blue cheese usually has a strong taste and should be used in moderation so as not to overshadow the other ingredients' flavors.

nuts and dried fruit

Nuts, such as almonds, walnuts, and pistachios, and dried fruit, such as raisins, dates, and prunes, add an important variety of flavors and textures to salads. I like adding nuts to salads because the crunch of an almond, the creaminess of a piece of cheese, and the sweetness of fruit create an irresistible combination. As with all ingredients in a salad, the key is to use just enough to balance with the other components.

grains

Grains come in various shapes, sizes, and colors, which not only add plenty of texture but also enhance the presentation of the salad. The most common grains are corn, wheat, rice, and quinoa.

dressings

Dressings are a world of their own! With a great variety of hues and flavors, they add even more flavor and depth to a beautiful mix of leaves and vegetables. To truly understand the importance of dressings, think of them as the connecting line uniting the flavors of a salad's every leaf, vegetable, cheese, nut, and herb. A simple salad with few ingredients can be exceptional with a good dressing.

We can classify dressings into three well-known groups: creamy dressings, vinaigrettes, and chunky dressings. All of them have specific characteristics that make them the perfect companions to certain salads.

- **Creamy dressings:** As the name suggests, these tend to be white dressings made of cream, mayonnaise, sour cream, or yogurt, along with other ingredients. The most popular ones include the Caesar and ranch dressings.

- **Vinaigrettes:** These dressings are mainly clear and light. They're based on an acidic component and oil, which gives them their characteristic texture. The most well-known ones are balsamic vinaigrette, mustard vinaigrette, and red wine vinaigrette.

- **Chunky dressings:** These dressings basically have the same base as vinaigrettes but are complemented with vegetables or finely chopped herbs to enhance their flavor and texture. The most common ones being garlic, onion, cilantro, parsley, and rosemary.

Although you can find a great variety of dressings from around the world at your supermarket, I suggest you make your dressings at home. There's nothing like a homemade dressing that is fresh and filled with high-quality ingredients and flavor. In this book, you'll find several recipes for outstanding dressings, so you can see the difference for yourself!

INGREDIENTS FOR A GOOD BASIC DRESSING

At my restaurants and at home, the rule I follow when making dressing is combining one part vinegar with two parts oil, although most chefs prefer one part vinegar and three parts oil. However, I find that the former combination makes a vinaigrette with better flavor and presence, resulting in a very pleasant balance when mixed with a salad. To enhance the flavors, add a pinch of salt and pepper and whisk all the ingredients in a bowl. Mix very well and for a good amount of time to make sure the ingredients don't separate. Another advantage of this basic dressing is that it can last a fairly long time in the refrigerator, unless you've added a dairy ingredient or herbs. If so, I recommend you don't keep it for more than one day.

how to combine flavors

The secret to creating a winning salad is in the combination of flavors and textures. Clearly, this will depend to some extent on your taste, but what follows is a guide based on my experience, so that you can create amazing combinations every time you make a salad.

In my case, I've always liked to mix sweet and savory flavors because there's a lot to gain with this combination. A perfect example is the delicious Watermelon, Tomato, and Feta Cheese Salad (page 139), in which the sweetness of the watermelon is enhanced by the saltiness of the feta cheese. I also find that playing around with textures can make a salad even more appetizing. You'll remember this when you try the delicious Grilled Seafood Salad with Avocado and Mango (page 122), in which I combine the avocado's creaminess with grilled shrimp. It will stun your guests.

> A simple salad with few ingredients can be exceptional with a good dressing.

Before we dive into the recipes, here are some final notes on dressings. Remember to add the dressing to the salad right before serving. If you add it any earlier, you will end up with a watery, soggy salad. Coat the leaves evenly to maintain a uniform flavor. One way to guarantee this is by mixing the salad with your (clean) hands. Carefully use your hands to turn and mix the salad, making sure every piece is covered by the delicious dressing.

Playing around with textures can make a salad even more appetizing.

chickpea and feta cheese salad

SERVES 4

This recipe is both delicious and super-nutritious. You can make it in very little time and it's ideal for any time of the year. This salad will keep you satisfied for a long time, since chickpeas, considered a legume, are full of fiber. It's fantastic served cold, and for vegetarians, it's a satisfying main dish.

INGREDIENTS:

    4 pieces pita bread

    olive oil

    1 red onion, chopped

    2 cloves garlic, minced

    ½ teaspoon cumin

    ½ teaspoon paprika

    ½ teaspoon cayenne pepper

    ½ pound chickpeas

    1 lemon, juice and zest

    1 tablespoon parsley, chopped

    4 ounces feta cheese

PREPARATION:

1. Brush the pita bread with olive oil, and toast it on both sides in a pan over medium heat.

2. In another pan over medium-high heat, add a drizzle of olive oil and sauté the onion, garlic, and spices. Add the chickpeas and continue sautéing. Add the lemon juice and zest and sauté for 2 more minutes. Immediately add the parsley, stir, and remove from the heat.

3. To finish, add a dash of olive oil and the feta cheese, and serve with the toasted pita bread.

quinoa and avocado salad

SERVES 4

The first time I heard about quinoa, a seed from countries including Peru and Bolivia, was in 2000. By 2005, quinoa had become a star superfood due to its nutritional value. It was preferred over and served in lieu of rice in restaurants and homes around the world. Although quinoa works well as a side dish, in this recipe, I've given it a bigger role and combined it with ingredients from another continent, creating a delicious fusion. The avocado's creaminess, the ginger's intensity and aroma, and the touch of cilantro take this salad's freshness to another level.

INGREDIENTS:

- 1 cup red quinoa
- 1 cup shelled edamame
- 1 cucumber, cut into small cubes
- 2 avocados, cubed
- 2 chives, chopped
- 2 tablespoons cilantro, chopped
- 1 teaspoon fresh ginger, minced
- 1 tablespoon sesame oil
- 2 tablespoons rice vinegar
- 2 tablespoons soy sauce

PREPARATION:

1. Combine the quinoa with 2 cups of water in a pot over high heat and bring to a boil. Reduce the heat, cover, and simmer for 15 minutes. Remove from the heat and let sit for 5 minutes.

2. Mix the rest of the ingredients in a large bowl.

3. After the quinoa has rested, add it to the bowl, mix the salad once more, and serve.

chef james tip >> **Rinse the quinoa before using to eliminate the powder that covers each seed and the bitter taste it gives off.**

grilled seafood salad with avocado and mango

SERVES 4

When my family and I moved to the United States, we worked very hard—seven days a week, many hours a day—to get ahead. During this time, we felt seafood was too expensive, until one day a good friend recommended that I visit a local fish market in Miami that was near the Miami River, where fresh seafood was available at reasonable prices. After finding this place, I started buying seafood on a regular basis and discovered how to prepare it. In this recipe, you will find flavors that are very much part of Latin America.

INGREDIENTS:

- ½ pound shrimp, peeled and deveined
- ½ pound squid (optional)
- ¼ pound mini scallops
- salt
- pepper
- olive oil
- 2 avocados
- 1 tomato, chopped
- 1 ripe mango, chopped
- 1 shallot, chopped
- 1 lemon, juice and zest
- cilantro, finely chopped
- 2 tablespoons white vinegar
- 1 dash hot sauce
- 1 tablespoon homemade mayonnaise

PREPARATION:

1. Season the seafood with salt, pepper, and olive oil and place it on a hot grill or pan. Cook for no more than 3 minutes, and remove from the heat.

2. Cut the avocados in half lengthwise and remove the pits.

3. In a glass bowl, mix the tomato, mango, shallot, lemon juice and zest, cilantro, vinegar, hot sauce, and mayonnaise.

4. Serve over the avocado halves.

niçoise salad

If you aren't sure how to pronounce the name of this dish, it's *neeswaz*—a traditional French salad from the city of Nice. When I first had Niçoise, I honestly didn't understand it, since each ingredient was served separately. Tomatoes, onions, olives, canned tuna—it just didn't make sense to me. For this recipe, I've created a modern version by maintaining the traditional elements while giving it my own personal touch. Remember to use fresh ingredients, and if you plan on refrigerating it and serving it later, make sure you don't add the dressing until right before you serve it so as to keep it fresh longer.

INGREDIENTS:

3 fresh tuna fillets

1 can black Kalamata olives

1 can green olives with pits

2 tablespoons capers, chopped

½ pound cherry tomatoes, halved

olive oil

salt

pepper

½ lemon

¼ cup Italian parsley, chopped, for garnish

PREPARATION:

1. In a pan or on an indoor grill over high heat, sear the tuna fillets.

2. Combine the olives, capers, and tomatoes in a bowl. Season with olive oil, salt, pepper, and a squeeze of lemon juice.

3. Remove the tuna from the grill, top it with the olive-tomato mixture, and garnish with the parsley.

fennel and salmon salad with honey vinaigrette

SERVES 4

This is one of the first salads I made on TV, striking and easy to put together. The fennel gives off a light anise flavor, which combines well with salmon. If you have time, you can toast the fennel in a pan to enhance its flavor. Everyone loved it on the show and I'm sure this recipe will liven up your taste buds at home.

INGREDIENTS:

¾ pound salmon

½ pound arugula

1 tablespoon red onion, chopped

1 zucchini, shaved into thin ribbons with a peeler

1 whole fennel

zest of 1 lemon

1 tablespoon fresh dill, finely chopped

salt

pepper

¼ cup olive oil

1 tablespoon white vinegar

2 tablespoons honey

juice of ½ lemon

¼ cup almonds, sliced and toasted

PREPARATION:

1. Cut the salmon into 1-inch cubes and in a pan or on an indoor grill over high heat, quickly sear, leaving the inside raw.

2. In a bowl, mix the arugula, red onion, zucchini, fennel, lemon zest and fresh dill.

3. In a separate bowl, whisk together the salt, pepper, olive oil, vinegar, honey, and lemon juice.

4. Pour the dressing over the salad and top with the almonds and the seared salmon cubes. Serve immediately.

chicken, arugula, and crouton salad

SERVES 4

Whenever I ordered a salad at a restaurant and it arrived filled to the brim with croutons, I always wondered, *Why buy a salad at a restaurant when I can make a better one at home?* For this salad, the croutons have a special role, while the chicken plays its own important part. The salad is mixed with a flavorful vinaigrette. This is one of those rustic homemade recipes I love!

INGREDIENTS:

FOR THE CHICKEN

5 deboned chicken thighs, with skin

1 cup arugula

FOR THE VINAIGRETTE

⅛ cup red wine vinegar

¼ cup olive oil

1 teaspoon Dijon mustard

1 clove garlic, minced

FOR THE CROUTONS

1 pound old rye bread

½ cup olive oil

2 tablespoons dried oregano

2 tablespoons dried thyme

2 tablespoons dried rosemary

2 tablespoons dried basil

pepper

2 tablespoons garlic powder

salt

¼ cup almonds, sliced and toasted

PREPARATION:

1. Preheat the oven to 375°F.

2. Place the chicken thighs on a medium-size baking tray and season with salt and pepper. Roast the chicken in the oven for 25 minutes. Take the tray out and let the chicken cool, making sure to save the remaining chicken juice.

3. Toss the chicken with the arugula.

4. To make the vinaigrette, whisk together the vinegar, oil, mustard, and garlic in a bowl. Set aside.

5. To make the croutons, preheat the oven to 400°F.

6. Cut the bread into 1-inch squares. In a bowl mix the olive oil with the herbs, pepper, garlic powder, and salt. Place the bread in a bowl, drizzle with the seasoned olive oil. Then place the bread on a baking tray and leave it in the oven for 12 to 15 minutes, or until the bread is toasted and hard.

7. Toss the arugula and chicken salad with the dressing.

8. Top with the croutons and sliced almonds.

hearts of palm salad

Traveling the world, I've noticed similarities among different cultures, even those that are thousands of miles apart. One of those similarities is the food. At home, when I was a child, we used to grill on Sundays, and hearts of palm were the salad staple. Although it's an ingredient produced mainly in South America, hearts of palm are consumed around the world, so you won't have trouble finding them at your local supermarket. I had always eaten them at restaurants or family members' homes, but to my surprise, during one of my trips to Mexico, at a street food stand, I was served a salad, in a plastic cup, that was exactly like the one my mom and dad made at home. It just goes to show that food has no boundaries and people's ingenuity never ceases to amaze us.

INGREDIENTS:

¼ cup sherry vinegar

1 teaspoon Dijon mustard

1 clove garlic, smashed

½ cup olive oil

salt

pepper

1 onion, chopped

3 tomatoes, diced

2 cups hearts of palm, sliced in rounds

¼ cup parsley, finely chopped

¼ cup cilantro, finely chopped

PREPARATION:

1. In a small bowl, combine the vinegar, mustard, and smashed garlic clove, and whisk with a fork. While whisking, slowly add the olive oil to make a creamy vinaigrette. Season with salt and pepper.

2. In a large bowl, combine the onion, tomatoes, hearts of palm, parsley, and cilantro.

3. Toss with the vinaigrette and serve.

warm corn salad

SERVES 2

This salad is unconventional because it's warm, and it is truly tasty. Additionally, it's so easy to make that it's ideal to prepare with the little ones at home as a shared kitchen activity. I love to prepare this recipe on the weekend, in the backyard, with the grill on. The grill's iron chars the corn wonderfully, concentrating its flavor and giving it a smoky touch that mixes perfectly with the rest of the ingredients.

INGREDIENTS:

4 ears corn, shucked

1 tomato, diced

1 roasted pepper, chopped

½ red onion, chopped

3 chive sprigs, finely chopped

½ pound Mexican cheese, diced

1 serrano chile, chopped

2 tablespoons cilantro, chopped

FOR THE VINAIGRETTE

2 cloves garlic, smashed

½ cup olive oil

1 tablespoon Dijon mustard

juice of 3 limes

PREPARATION:

1. Grill the ears of corn for 20 minutes. Turn every minute. Remove from the grill, and using a towel to hold the hot cobs, and cut the kernels off the cob.

2. In a bowl, combine the corn with the tomato, pepper, onion, chives, cheese, chile, and cilantro.

3. To make the vinaigrette, in a blender, mix all of the vinaigrette ingredients for 2 minutes.

4. Toss the salad with the vinaigrette to taste, and serve.

caprese salad with portobello mushrooms

SERVES 4

Once you've tried this recipe, you will never again eat the conventional caprese salad. The portobello mushrooms add great texture without affecting the salad's refreshing taste. Also, the mushrooms add to the presentation; you'll look like a famous chef when serving it. It's perfect for a romantic dinner!

INGREDIENTS:

4 portobello mushrooms

½ cup balsamic vinegar

1 pound fresh buffalo mozzarella

1 bunch basil

2 tomatoes, cut into 1-inch round slices

PREPARATION:

1. Preheat the oven to 350°F.

2. Put the portobello mushrooms on a baking tray and cook for 7 minutes. Remove from the oven and let them sit for 10 minutes.

3. In a pot over medium heat, reduce the balsamic vinegar until it reaches the consistency of a glaze or syrup.

4. To serve, arrange the ingredients in four small towers by stacking the mushrooms, mozzarella, basil and tomato. Finish with the glazed vinegar.

chef james tip >> When choosing a portobello mushroom, make sure its outer layer is dry and firm. If it has very soft parts, then it's not fresh.

watermelon, tomato, and feta cheese salad

SERVES 4

This is one of the most refreshing salads I have ever had. It is perfect to eat while sitting in your backyard on a hot day. Also, this recipe will open your senses and expose your palate to new flavor combinations. Adding watermelon to regular salad ingredients such as tomato and feta cheese gives this recipe an unprecedented flavor. You can also prepare it quickly after a long workday and serve it for dinner.

INGREDIENTS:

2 tomatoes, diced

1 cup diced watermelon

½ red onion, julienned

½ cup feta cheese, crumbled

2 tablespoons basil, chopped

2 tablespoons mint, chopped

salt

pepper

2 to 3 tablespoons olive oil

juice of 1 lemon

PREPARATION:

1. In a bowl, combine the tomatoes, watermelon, onion, feta, basil, and mint, and season with salt and pepper.

2. Add the olive oil and lemon juice, mix well, and serve.

warm artichoke and chile salad with grapefruit vinaigrette

SERVES 4

You'll be surprised by the burst of flavor in this delicious salad. This is not your typical boring lettuce, tomato, and onion salad that's served everywhere. We're creating flavors here! The grapefruit vinaigrette's acidity together with the artichoke's unique flavor make for an unforgettable combination that you can prepare at home in very little time. Additionally, since it's warm, it brings the salad world into another dimension.

INGREDIENTS:

4 tablespoons olive oil, plus more for the pan

3 red chiles, chopped

1 pound artichoke hearts

3 chives, chopped

4 tablespoons olive oil

juice of 1 lemon

juice of 1 grapefruit

1 teaspoon Dijon mustard

½ red onion, chopped

20 red and yellow cherry tomatoes, halved

10 slices grapefruit, peeled

PREPARATION:

1. In a pan over medium-high heat, add a drizzle of oil and sauté the chiles, artichoke hearts, and chives for 2 minutes. Remove from heat.

2. In a blender, combine the 4 tablespoons of olive oil and the lemon juice, grapefruit juice, and mustard, and blend until smooth.

3. In a bowl, mix the sautéed artichoke heart mixture with the dressing and add the onion, cherry tomatoes, and grapefruit slices and serve.

Bistec
Kuu ya kozi
Main Course
Steak
Plato Principal
Pollo
Zhǔ cài
huvudrätt

main dishes

We've reached what many believe to be the climax of food. After all, the role of all the previous dishes is to prepare for the recipes in this section. Also known as entrées or main courses, these dishes are the most satiating part of a meal and are usually made up of meat, vegetables, or a good plate of pasta or risotto.

Each dish within a full-course meal is a fantastic opportunity to impress anyone, but when it comes down to it, the main dish is usually the one that brings a chef the most praise. I think this is because in most cases, main dishes are made with a world-class approach, so much so that if the dish is exceptional, it can even become a country's national treasure. That's how powerful food is! Think about it: Who can think of paella without thinking of Spain? Pot-au-feu and crepes without thinking of France? Tacos and mole without thinking of Mexico?

Despite the fact that the main dish is usually the most elaborate, you shouldn't feel intimidated when it comes time to prepare it. On the contrary, get excited that you'll soon be showered with praise; think how much you will impress yourself as well as your guests. For this section, I've chosen a variety of recipes so you can frequently make different dishes—most are superfast to make without sacrificing flavor. I divided them into three sections so that you can easily find the dishes you're craving. Finally, I included information that will be incredibly valuable to you when getting ready to make these recipes! Let's get moving!

land

In the beginning of the book, I explained how to choose the best primal cuts and fresh meat at the supermarket and butcher shop. Before you venture into cooking these delicious dishes, you should know the basics of cooking meat properly.

To better understand how to cook meat, it's important to learn the different primal cuts and what cooking methods will most enhance their flavors. Each cut of meat has its own texture; for example, shoulders, tails, and chuck are from muscle that the animal uses frequently; therefore, these parts tend to be tough. The best way to soften these cuts is to slow cook them over a long period of time. Roasting in the oven and using a slow cooker are the most popular methods. Although it takes a little patience, the wait and long cooking time are well rewarded when the once tough and fibrous piece of meat melts in your mouth. Slow cooking is one of my favorite ways to cook meat.

On the other hand, the cuts that come from the back are usually the most tender since the animal hardly uses the muscles in that part of its body. Among these are the loin, beefsteak, and T-bone steak. Each one of these cuts tends to be cooked faster as fillets and can even be served slightly rare, depending on a person's taste. Recommended cooking methods include on the grill, on the griddle, or fried in oil or butter in a pan. If you aren't going to marinate these cuts before cooking, I recommend that you salt them after you've cooked them. If you salt beforehand, the salt will dehydrate the meat as it cooks, making it dry rather than juicy.

Chicken is very versatile, and since it's not that tough, it can be cooked however you please.

I'm a meat lover, and if I had to choose, I'd pick the tough, fibrous, cheaper cuts. Every minute the meat spends cooking makes it that much more incredible. However, if you're in a rush or if you are cooking with meat during the week, I recommend choosing tender cuts. They are easier to handle and they cook faster, which will allow you to make more efficient use of your time in the kitchen and at home. For these reasons, I've included tender cuts of meat in most of my recipes.

meat terminology

Some like their beef rare and others enjoy it well-done. Either way, if you plan on cooking steaks at home, it's a good idea to familiarize yourself with the different degrees of doneness in meat. It's especially useful if you are cooking for more than yourself and if you plan on entertaining guests, whether for a barbecue or a sumptuous dinner.

Remember, before the meat is cooked, it must be thawed and brought to room temperature. This will help the meat cook uniformly throughout. If you're going to marinate it, I recommend you do so while it's raw.

Each dish within a full-course meal is a fantastic opportunity to impress anyone.

- **Rare:** A piece of meat that is cooked rare is well seared on both sides, while the inside is still rare. It usually takes around 3 minutes for each side to cook to this degree of doneness. The temperature at the cut's center should be around 131°F and the color at the center should be bright red. The meat's texture is tender, but it's important to note that this temperature is used mainly for low-fat cuts since fat won't reach its melting point at this level of doneness and could remain solid.

- **Medium:** This is my favorite! It'll take you about 6 minutes on each side to cook the meat to this degree. At this level of doneness, the temperature at the center should be 145°F and the color at the center pinkish red. You'll notice its texture is slightly resistant.

- **Medium-well:** Many people prefer this degree of doneness because it maintains a firm consistency, without being too tough, and with no blood residue. To achieve this level of doneness you'll usually have to cook the meat for around 8 minutes on each side. You'll notice that the interior color here will be light brown, while the temperature in the middle will be 150°F.

- **Well-done:** This is also known in several Latin American countries as *suela de zapato* (sole of a shoe), or leathery meat, because it loses most of its juiciness and its texture becomes very tough. Its classic color is gray and the temperature in the center is around 158°F. It'll take you between 10 and 12 minutes per side to cook a cut of meat to this degree of doneness. It's the degree I least recommend for grilled cuts of meat.

Now that you know a bit more about meat, it's time you put theory into practice. Don't forget to cook with lots of passion, and don't be afraid of making mistakes!

ground turkey lettuce wraps

SERVES 4

One of the things we often hear is that healthy food is boring and bland. This recipe ends that myth! The crispy iceberg lettuce combined with the concentrated soy sauce perfectly complements the turkey's texture and flavor. It's my go-to recipe when I want to eat a flavorful and healthy meal in minutes.

INGREDIENTS:

½ onion, finely chopped

2 ounces mushrooms

1 tablespoon garlic, minced

½ pound ground turkey

2 tablespoons soy sauce

1 tablespoon rice vinegar

1 head iceberg lettuce, leaves separated and washed

PREPARATION:

1. In a pan over high heat, sauté the onion and mushrooms. Add the garlic and turkey and season with the soy sauce and vinegar. Cook until the turkey is browned.

2. Serve the turkey in the lettuce-leaf cups.

steak with cream and pepper sauce (steak au poivre)

SERVES 2

This recipe has stood the test of time in my repertoire. It's a classic French recipe that I believe is the embodiment of high-quality fast food. The steak's tender texture together with the sauce's creaminess will make anyone's mouth water. Best of all, you can make it from start to finish in just 10 minutes.

INGREDIENTS:

2 thick steaks (preferably New York strip)
¼ cup Worcestershire sauce
1 cup heavy cream
green peppercorns

PREPARATION:

1. In a cast-iron pan over high heat, sear the steaks until the outer layer is crispy or reaches the desired doneness (see pages 145–46). Remove from heat and let them rest in a separate container.

2. Cook the Worcestershire sauce in the same pan over high heat and reduce it by ¼. Add the cream and peppercorns. Reduce again by half, and add the steaks to the pan over high heat. Let sit for 2 minutes and serve.

chef james tip >> Before adding to heat, let the steaks rest at room temperature to guarantee that they're at the optimum temperature for searing. Doing so will help maintain the high temperature of the pan once the meat is added.

neapolitan meatballs

SERVES 6

This recipe is a perfect example of one of those rustic dishes you can serve in the middle of the table and eat with your family—a delicacy worthy of the best Italian kitchens. I've added a couple of tips that will help you save a good chunk of time while making this dish. Let me warn you that in my home they love it when I make this recipe and they always ask for second helpings, so get ready because you'll likely be in the same boat.

INGREDIENTS:

FOR THE MEATBALLS

2 pounds ground beef

2 eggs

4 cloves garlic, minced

¼ cup olive oil

1 cup Italian bread crumbs

½ cup Pecorino Romano cheese

¼ cup toasted pine nuts

2 tablespoons parsley, finely chopped

FOR THE MARINARA SAUCE

½ cup olive oil

2 onions, finely chopped

2 cloves garlic, minced

2 carrots, finely diced

2 stalks celery, finely chopped

4 bay leaves

2 chipotle chiles, blended

2 32-ounce cans crushed tomatoes

1 cup water

PREPARATION:

1. Preheat the oven to 450°F.

2. To make the meatballs, mix all the ingredients well in a bowl. Do this by adding a few at a time, mixing well after every few additions.

3. Shape the mixture into golf ball–size meatballs and arrange on a baking tray lined with aluminum foil. Place the tray in the oven and cook for 20 minutes, until the meatballs are browned.

4. Meanwhile, make the marinara sauce. In a pot over medium-high heat, add the olive oil and sauté the onions and garlic until the onions turn translucent. Add the carrots and celery and cook for 4 minutes.

5. Add the bay leaves, chipotles, tomatoes, and water. Cook for 30 minutes over medium-high heat to concentrate the flavors. Add the meatballs to the sauce and cook for another 15 minutes.

chef james tip >> Making the meatballs in the oven shaves about 20 minutes from this recipe's prep time. You would normally brown them in batches in a pan, constantly stirring them; however, using the oven instead makes this a much easier, fast, and convenient step.

pepper steak and hoisin sauce

SERVES 4

You need only a few ingredients to prepare a dish exactly like the one you get at your corner Chinese restaurant. The meat's flavor is complemented well with the hoisin sauce, a frequently used condiment in Asian gastronomy that combines sweet, spicy, and savory flavors. Nowadays you can find hoisin sauce anywhere, but it's an intensely flavored sauce, so use it in small quantities. What's good about this recipe is that since it's easy and fast to make, you can do so any day of the week. Lack of time can no longer be used as an excuse for not eating well!

INGREDIENTS:

olive oil

1 pound skirt steak, cut in strips

2 green peppers, cut in strips

2 cloves garlic, minced

2 tablespoons sesame oil

1 onion, thinly sliced

6 tablespoons hoisin sauce

PREPARATION:

1. In a pan over high heat, add a dash of olive oil and brown the meat on all sides.

2. Then add the rest of the ingredients, except the hoisin sauce, and sauté for a couple of minutes.

3. Finally, add the hoisin sauce, stir, and turn the heat off. Let it sit and serve.

chef james tip >> To cook meat more uniformly and to ensure that it has better texture, flip the steak every 15 to 30 seconds. Don't cook it only on one side and then the other because you will create a tough outer layer.

almond-crusted chicken

SERVES 4

This recipe came about during the many fishing trips I took with my friends a few years back. Before we took off, we always made the traditional breaded chicken, which, if eaten regularly, can put on the pounds given the amount of oil and bread used to prepare it. After several fishing trips, smack in the middle of the open sea, I wondered, *How can I make this breaded chicken healthier without losing its crunch?* And a light that triggered this recipe went on in my head.

INGREDIENTS:

juice of 4 oranges

4 cloves garlic, minced

1 habanero chile, punctured

½ onion, finely chopped

1 teaspoon soy sauce

4 thin chicken breasts

1 cup whole wheat flour

3 eggs, beaten

2 cups almonds, finely processed

PREPARATION:

1. Preheat the oven to 375°F.

2. To make the marinade, in a bowl combine the orange juice, garlic, chile, onion, and soy sauce. Add the chicken breasts to the marinade, cover the bowl with plastic wrap, and place it in the refrigerator for 4 hours.

3. After the chicken is marinated, lay out three plates and put the flour on one, the eggs on the second, and the ground almonds on the last. Coat a chicken breast in the flour, then the egg, and finally the almonds, setting it on an aluminum foil–lined baking tray. Transfer the tray to the oven and cook for 35 minutes.

> **chef james tip >>** To obtain a more rustic texture, don't thoroughly process some of the almonds. This will leave slightly bigger pieces that will make your crust incredibly crunchy.

roasted chicken with shallot and herb vinaigrette

Few things are as easy in the kitchen as roasting a chicken! Okay, maybe that is a slight exaggeration, but this recipe will truly make it far easier to make. Roasted chicken oftentimes carries with it the bad reputation of having dry chicken breasts, but in this case not only will we cook it perfectly, but we'll also give it an extra touch of flavor with an extremely aromatic vinaigrette. The result will be a dish that looks and tastes amazing.

INGREDIENTS:

1 whole chicken

olive oil

salt

pepper

1 head garlic, cut in half

3 sprigs thyme

3 sprigs rosemary

2 lemons, cut in half

FOR THE VINAIGRETTE

½ cup olive oil

⅛ cup red wine vinegar

1 shallot, finely chopped

2 tablespoons parsley, finely chopped

1 tablespoon thyme, finely chopped

zest of 1 lemon

PREPARATION:

1. Preheat the oven to 375°F.

2. Season the whole chicken with olive oil, salt, and pepper. Rub the cut sides of the garlic on the chicken and stuff the garlic, herbs, and lemons inside the chicken cavity. Place the chicken in a roasting pan in the oven, and roast for 45 minutes.

3. Remove the chicken and set aside.

4. In a bowl, whisk together the vinaigrette ingredients.

5. Season the chicken with the vinaigrette or serve the vinaigrette on the side.

chicken piccata

SERVES 4

This is a great recipe to kick off your journey as a home chef. It's easy to make and has a refreshing flavor. Chicken piccata is one of the most popular dishes in restaurants around the world. Prepared in my style, it becomes a perfect fast food. And when I say "fast food," it's because of how simple it is to make and how little time you need, not because it is in any way similar to the quality of the food served in fast-food restaurants. Finally, you'll find that this dish has a perfect balance of creaminess from the butter and citrus from the lemon that will make your guests' mouths water.

INGREDIENTS:

4 chicken breasts, pounded thin

salt

pepper

olive oil

2 shallots, finely chopped

1 clove garlic, minced

2 tablespoons capers

¼ cup sherry

1 cup chicken broth

juice of 2 lemons

1 tablespoon cold butter

1 tablespoon parsley, finely chopped

lemon wedges

PREPARATION:

1. Season the chicken breasts with salt and pepper.

2. In a pan, add a dash of olive oil and brown the chicken over high heat until golden brown. Remove the chicken from the pan and transfer to a plate.

3. In the same pan, sauté the shallots, garlic, and capers over medium-high heat. Once the aromatics are tender, add the sherry and reduce by half, then add the broth and reduce by half. Add the lemon juice and finish the sauce with the cold butter.

4. Return the chicken breasts to the pan with the sauce and finish with the parsley. Serve, garnished with the lemon wedges.

main dishes

chicken teriyaki

SERVES 4

Chicken teriyaki is one of the most popular Asian dishes. It is simple, delicious, and very easy to make, and although everyone has their own version of this recipe, I find that it works best when it's made in a slow cooker. This method helps richen and seal in the flavors so that each bite is a magical experience. I also like using the slow cooker because the prep time is minimal, and then I can forget about it for around 5 hours, until it's ready to eat.

INGREDIENTS:

- 1 pound skinless, boneless chicken thighs
- 4 tablespoons soy sauce
- 3 cloves garlic, smashed
- 3 tablespoons ginger, finely chopped
- 2 tablespoons brown sugar
- 2 tablespoons sake
- 1 teaspoon rice vinegar
- 1 red pepper, chopped
- 1 green pepper, chopped
- 1 onion, chopped
- 2 carrots, diced
- 1 cup white rice, cooked
- chives, chopped, for garnish

PREPARATION:

1. Mix all the ingredients except the chives in a slow cooker and cook for 4 to 5 hours, until the chicken literally falls apart as it comes out of the cooker.

2. Serve the chicken in a deep dish so that people can help themselves. Place the chives in a small serving container for garnishing.

twelve spices grilled chicken

SERVES 4

This is another recipe that was on one of my restaurant's summer menus, when it's all about grilling. It holds an incredible amount of flavor since the spices become a delicious crust. On top of that, what will steal the show, aside from the chef, of course, is the vinaigrette, which gives it the perfect creamy finishing touch.

INGREDIENTS:

1 tablespoon ancho chile powder

1 tablespoon cumin

1 tablespoon smoked paprika

1 tablespoon black pepper, plus more for the vinaigrette

1 tablespoon ground allspice

1 tablespoon ground cinnamon

½ teaspoon ground clove

1 tablespoon garlic powder

1 tablespoon onion powder

1 tablespoon ground oregano

1 tablespoon ground thyme

1 tablespoon sugar

3 teaspoons salt, plus more for the vinaigrette

4 chicken breasts

4 teaspoons vinegar

8 tablespoons olive oil plus more for the pan

1 teaspoon mustard

3 chive sprigs, cut lengthwise, for garnish

microgreens, for garnish

PREPARATION:

1. Mix all the spices and herbs, the sugar, and 3 teaspoons of the salt in a bowl.

2. Season the chicken breasts with the spice mix.

3. On a grill or in a pan with a dash of olive oil over high heat, cook the breasts for 3 to 4 minutes on each side or until the insides are fully cooked and juicy.

4. Combine the vinegar, 8 tablespoons of oil, mustard, and salt and pepper to taste in a blender to make a vinaigrette. Spoon the vinaigrette over the cooked chicken.

5. Garnish with the chives and microgreens.

chicken with artichokes, olives, and capers in a white wine sauce

SERVES 4

This was the first dish I made in culinary school, following the instructions I found on YouTube. When I came upon this video, I liked the recipe so much that I had to try it. My version is a perfect guide and yet flexible enough that you can try different variations. At the same time, this dish is also very simple to make, and it creates a festival of flavors in your mouth.

INGREDIENTS:

4 skinless, boneless chicken thighs

salt

pepper

olive oil

1 shallot, finely chopped

1 tomato, diced

4 ounces artichoke, cut into fourths

2 ounces Kalamata olives

2 tablespoons capers

1 cup white wine

parsley, chopped, for garnish

PREPARATION:

1. Season the chicken with salt and pepper.

2. In a pan, add a splash of olive oil and warm over medium-high heat. Brown the chicken in the pan, remove, and transfer to a plate.

3. In the same pan, sauté the shallot with the tomato, artichoke, olives, and capers. Deglaze the pan with the white wine and reduce until the wine has a thick consistency.

4. Return the chicken to the pan and let it simmer in the sauce.

5. Serve, garnished with the parsley.

chicken breast stuffed with sun-dried tomatoes and feta cheese

SERVES 2

I made this recipe on TV one day in response to social network comments that said chicken breasts tend to be boring and dry. Seeing this as a challenge, I sliced a chicken breast in half and stuffed it with ingredients that would add flavor, texture, and juiciness to the final product. There's nothing better than wild rice to accompany this dish, but if you don't have any handy, white rice will also do the trick.

INGREDIENTS:

  1 cup sun-dried tomatoes in oil, finely chopped

  1 clove garlic, minced

  1 cup feta cheese, crumbled

  salt

  pepper

  4 tablespoons fresh oregano, finely chopped

  4 tablespoons fresh basil, finely chopped

  2 chicken breasts, with skin, boneless

  olive oil

  1 cup wild rice, cooked, as a side dish

PREPARATION:

1. Preheat the oven to 400°F.

2. In a bowl, mix the sun-dried tomatoes with the garlic, feta cheese, salt, pepper, oregano, and basil.

3. Pound the chicken breasts with a kitchen hammer until they're about 2 inches thick. Make an incision in the middle of each piece, creating a type of pocket by letting the knife run from top to bottom on the thickest side.

4. Stuff 2 tablespoons of the tomato-feta mixture in each of the chicken breasts.

5. Wrap each stuffed chicken breast in aluminum foil and place it in the refrigerator for 20 minutes.

6. Preheat a pan and add a splash of olive oil. Remove the chicken from the refrigerator and unwrap the foil. Place the chicken breasts in the pan until they are golden brown. Be careful when handling the chicken so that the stuffing doesn't fall out.

7. Remove the chicken from the pan. Place on a baking tray and place inside the oven. Bake for 20 to 25 minutes.

8. Serve over the wild rice.

chef james tip >> Make sure your knife is sharp to make a finer and more accurate incision in the chicken breasts when creating the pockets.

Every minute the meat
spends cooking makes it
that much more incredible.

reina pepiada arepa
(arepa filled with chicken, avocado, and mayonnaise)

SERVES 6

This is one of the most well-known and delicious dishes from my country, Venezuela. You can easily serve it for breakfast, lunch, or dinner. *Reina pepiada* refers to the arepa's filling, made of boiled chicken mixed with avocados and a touch of mayonnaise. I used to have them at the *areperas* we found along the highways, and nowadays it's one of my go-to recipes to enjoy with my family on Sundays because it's so quick to make.

INGREDIENTS:

2 chicken breasts, boiled and shredded

½ onion, finely chopped

2 Hass avocados, mashed

¼ cup mayonnaise

1 tablespoon lemon juice

3 tablespoons cilantro, chopped

3 tablespoons chives, chopped

salt

pepper

1 pound Harina P.A.N. (precooked cornmeal)

PREPARATION:

1. Mix all the ingredients in a bowl, except the cornmeal, and season with salt and pepper.

2. Make the arepas following the instructions on the Harina P.A.N. package. Once they're ready, split them open and fill them with the reina pepiada mixture.

chef james tip >> If you're trying to cut back on the carbs, I recommend that you make very thin arepas. The dough simply holds the filling, and you won't lose any flavor.

carne asada tacos

Whenever I travel far from home, I like to eat at popular spots. And I'm not necessarily referring to popular tourist places (I avoid them), but rather to places that are frequented by the locals. I ask for their recommendations and let them guide me. If they are regulars at these places, then they must know the best food spots in town. I don't think I've ever had better tacos than the ones I tried from the small street stands in Mexico, and that's what inspired this dish. What makes this recipe is the marinade. I changed it up a bit to quicken the process, so that you can enjoy it in less time without sacrificing the flavor.

INGREDIENTS:

1 pound skirt steak

juice of 3 lemons

1 tablespoon Worcestershire sauce

½ onion, chopped

½ tablespoon oregano, finely chopped

½ tablespoon cumin

4 tablespoons olive oil

black pepper

8 corn tortillas

¼ cup cilantro, chopped

PREPARATION:

1. Place the meat in a large Ziploc bag. Add the lemon juice, Worcestershire sauce, onion, oregano, cumin, and a dash of the olive oil and black pepper. Let the meat marinate for 15 minutes and then cook in a pan with olive oil or on a hot griddle until the desired inside temperature is reached. Remove the meat and let it rest for 5 minutes.

2. In the same pan, heat the tortillas over medium heat until they're warm. Serve with cilantro.

cuban sandwich

Nothing is more emblematic of Miami than the Cuban sandwich. It's pure heaven between two pieces of bread. As a product of the many Cuban immigrants in South Florida, these classic sandwiches are sold at many small stands, and, like vendors everywhere, the stands compete to see who makes the best in the city. The real winners are those of us who try them. The secret is in the pork marinade, the main reason your Cuban sandwich will have different levels of flavor. Here's a version with a summary of what I think works best for this distinguished dish. You won't believe that something that takes so little time to make can be so delicious!

INGREDIENTS:

juice of 1 lemon

juice of 1 orange

1 teaspoon cumin

1 teaspoon oregano

⅛ cup olive oil

1 pound pork loin, cut in ½-inch slices

2 tablespoons butter

4 to 6 rolls Cuban bread or ciabatta

4 tablespoons mustard

4 pickles, sliced in rounds

8 slices Swiss cheese

1 pound ham, sliced

PREPARATION:

1. Mix the lemon and orange juice, cumin, oregano, and olive oil in a bowl.

2. Add the pork and let it marinate for 15 minutes in the refrigerator. Once marinated, place in a pan over medium heat and cook until browned. Remove from the heat.

3. To make the sandwiches, spread about ½ tablespoon butter on the outside of each roll. On one half of each roll, spread the mustard, then stack the pickles, cheese, ham, and pork. Set the other half of the roll on top. Toast each sandwich on both sides over medium heat, placing a pan on top of the sandwich as it toasts to flatten it. Do this until it is toasted. Cut each sandwich in half and serve.

chef james tip >>
For this recipe, you can also use leftover pork. Just add the rest of the ingredients, season, and you're done!

milanesa sandwich

This quick, classic dish brings Argentina to your kitchen. It's perfect when you're in a rush and don't have much time to cook. It's also great for kids since usually they will eat most anything in the shape of a sandwich, and so it's also a great way to feed them some veggies. For this recipe, I add tomato and lettuce, but if you're feeling creative at home, you can add countless other vegetables.

INGREDIENTS:

1 cup corn or peanut oil for frying

4 steaks of 4 to 6 ounces and ½-inch thick each

salt

pepper

½ cup flour

2 eggs, beaten

1 cup bread crumbs

4 baguettes

4 tablespoons mustard

4 tablespoons mayonnaise

1 tomato, sliced in rounds

1 head romaine lettuce

1 lemon, cut into fourths

PREPARATION:

1. Preheat the oil in a medium frying pan to 375°F.

2. Season the steaks with salt and pepper. Then set up a basic breading station by putting the flour in a plate, beaten eggs in another and bread crumbs in a third. Then coat the steaks with flour, eliminating any excess. Dip them in the beaten eggs and coat them with bread crumbs.

3. In the pan, fry each side of the steaks for 3 minutes. Remove from the heat and place on a plate. Slice open the bread and add mustard on one side and mayonnaise on the other. Into each baguette, place 1 milanesa steak, a couple of slices of tomato, and the lettuce. Serve with the lemon wedges.

main dishes

pork chops with roasted vegetables

SERVES 2

This is a dish that looks and tastes delicious—oven-roasted pork hardly ever disappoints. Best of all, you need just one baking tray to hold every ingredient. Each time I make these pork chops at home, my guests are delighted by the exquisiteness of the dish, and I know you will feel the same. I recommend that you make it for a weekend family lunch by multiplying the ingredients for whatever number of servings needed.

INGREDIENTS:

2 pork chops, bone in	pepper
6 fingerling potatoes	¼ cup red wine vinegar
2 tomatoes	1 cup chicken broth
1 onion	2 tablespoons parsley, chopped
1 head garlic	5 sprigs rosemary, finely chopped
olive oil	1 tablespoon Dijon mustard
salt	

PREPARATION:

1. Preheat the oven to 400°F.

2. Season the pork chops and vegetables with olive oil, salt, and pepper, and then place in the oven and roast for 40 minutes. Everything should look nice and brown. Then immediately remove from the oven and transfer the meat and vegetables to a bowl.

3. Into the same baking tray, pour the vinegar and chicken broth and add the parsley and rosemary. Cook on the stove top over high heat for 1 minute to lightly reduce the mixture. Add the mustard, mix well, and serve over the pork chops and vegetables.

chef james tip >> Place the empty baking tray in the oven while it's preheating. This will help sear and brown the pork chops and vegetables as soon as they come into contact with the tray, saving you some time.

chicken curry

Bring the delicious flavor of this Indian dish to your kitchen. If used correctly, curry will reward you with incredible flavor. I was very young when I first tried it, and I was fascinated by its intense aroma and taste. Soon after I began my culinary education, I discovered that, since it's such a strong ingredient, you need to watch how much you use so it doesn't overpower the other flavors. You'll be happy to know that although this recipe has many ingredients, it's easy to make. Better yet, you'll learn how to make a fresh and flavorful curry dish from scratch, just like I did when I was a kid. In case you didn't already know, curry is actually a mix of different spices—it can also be used with other proteins, such as fish, pork, and meat.

INGREDIENTS:

oil

1 onion, chopped

4 cloves garlic, minced

1 tablespoon fresh ginger, minced

½ tablespoon cayenne pepper

3 tablespoons curry powder or curry paste

1 teaspoon ground cinnamon

1 tablespoon smoked paprika

1 tablespoon sugar

2 chicken breasts, cubed

1 tablespoon tomato paste

1 cup yogurt

1 cup coconut milk

1 tablespoon lemongrass paste

juice of 1 lemon

2 tablespoons cilantro, chopped

2 tablespoons microgreens

2 cups cooked rice

PREPARATION:

1. In a large pot over medium-high heat, combine the oil, onion, garlic, and ginger and sauté for 2 minutes.

2. Add the cayenne pepper, curry powder, cinnamon, paprika, and sugar, and cook for another minute.

3. Add the chicken, tomato paste, yogurt, coconut milk, and lemongrass paste. Bring the mixture to a boil and reduce the heat to medium. Cook for 30 minutes and finish with the lemon juice.

4. Serve garnished with the cilantro and microgreens and the rice on the side.

main dishes

hamburgers *al pastor*

SERVES 4

This delicious hamburger will satisfy anyone's expectations, and since it's such a simple recipe to make, you'll have enough for seconds. Few things complement each other as well as pork and pineapple—you'll understand when you sink your teeth into this burger! The inspiration for this innovative recipe comes from the delicious and marvelous Mexican tacos *al pastor*.

INGREDIENTS:

- 4 guajillo chiles, rehydrated in water
- 1 tablespoon oregano
- 2 cloves garlic, minced
- salt
- pepper
- ½ onion, finely chopped
- ½ cup pineapple juice
- 1 pound ground pork
- 4 slices pineapple
- 6 tablespoons mayonnaise
- 4 hamburger rolls
- cilantro, chopped

PREPARATION:

1. Preheat an oiled pan or a grill over medium to high heat.

2. To make the al pastor sauce, in a blender, mix the chiles, oregano, garlic, salt, pepper, onion, and pineapple juice for 1 minute. Pour the sauce in a bowl together with the ground pork.

3. With your hands, combine the meat and sauce. To make the patties, roll ¼ of the seasoned ground meat into a ball and lightly press it between your hands or on a flat surface. Repeat with the rest of the meat mixture until you have 4 same-size patties.

4. Cook the patties on a grill or in a pan for 4 minutes on each side. Remove the patties and let them rest on a plate.

5. In the same pan or grill, brown the pineapple slices over medium heat for 5 minutes on each side.

6. Spread the mayonnaise on the inside of each bun, add the patty, then the pineapple, and sprinkle with the cilantro. Top with the other half of the bun and serve.

chef james tip >> If you have time, make the *al pastor* sauce a day ahead so that the flavors have time to fuse and integrate better. This will give the sauce a smoother consistency.

roasted chicken with lemon and cilantro sauce

SERVES 4 TO 6

I don't know many people who can resist a delicious roasted chicken. The crispy, perfectly golden brown skin and the aroma are a lethal combination—they cast a spell. I really like this particular recipe because the lemon and cilantro sauce gives the chicken a refreshing taste. It's also very special to me because it was a classic dish my dad used to cook. I'm including it in the book because I know it will become a staple in your home.

INGREDIENTS:

    1 cup cilantro

    ¼ cup olive oil

    ¾ tablespoon cumin

    ½ cup lemon juice

    3 tablespoons mustard

    5 cloves garlic

    lemon zest

    2 serrano chiles

    1 pound potatoes, sliced 1-inch thick

    6 skinless chicken thighs

PREPARATION:

1. Preheat the oven to 400°F. Once the oven is hot, place an empty ovenproof glass baking dish inside.

2. To make the cilantro sauce, in a blender, mix the cilantro, olive oil, cumin, lemon juice, mustard, garlic, lemon zest, and chiles for 1 minute.

3. Remove the baking dish from the oven, and arrange the sliced potatoes in the dish to form a bed for the chicken to rest on.

4. Place the chicken on top of the potatoes and pour the cilantro sauce over the chicken.

5. Bake in the oven for 1 hour.

pork stewed in honey

SERVES 8 TO 10

This unique dish's prep time is minimal. All the magic that gives flavor to this recipe happens during the 2 hours it cooks in the oven, where the flavors fuse together and the honey settles into the pork. The incredible taste of the finished stew is the final reward for the wait. If you follow my steps, I guarantee you'll have the wow factor in this dish!

INGREDIENTS:

2 pounds pork for stew, cut into pieces

5 cloves garlic

1 ginger root

1 tablespoon red peppercorns

1 tablespoon black pepper

1 tablespoon star anise

¼ cup honey

3 tablespoons soy sauce

2 tablespoons rice vinegar

1 cup sake

1 cup chicken broth

2 tablespoons cilantro, finely chopped

PREPARATION:

1. Preheat the oven to 350°F.

2. In a stovetop-safe baking tray over a burner on high heat, cook the pork until golden brown on all sides. Add the rest of the ingredients, except the cilantro, stir to combine, and place in the oven to cook for 2 hours.

3. Remove from the oven and serve garnished with the cilantro.

chef james tip >>
You can use any leftover pork the next day to make delicious sandwiches with mustard and salt on toasted bread. The honey-flavored pork goes really well with mustard and crunchy bread. And that's how easy it is to have another delicious meal in minutes!

flank steak with coffee crust and salsa criolla

SERVES 4

Many of us see coffee only as a source of caffeine; however, this recipe will give you a new take on this aromatic ingredient. This is a dish that will get you out of your usual routine, and the flavor is worth the time it takes to make. Not only does coffee go perfectly with the tender flank, but roasting it also creates a crispy crust that, combined with the salsa criolla, gives this recipe the wow factor.

INGREDIENTS:

2 pounds beef brisket

FOR THE COFFEE CRUST

1½ tablespoons ancho chile powder

1½ tablespoons ground coffee

½ tablespoon brown sugar

¼ tablespoon dried mustard

¼ tablespoon salt

¼ tablespoon black pepper

FOR THE SALSA CRIOLLA

1 onion, finely chopped

2 chives, chopped

1 tomato, diced

½ cup olive oil

¼ cup vinegar

⅛ teaspoon cumin

½ red pepper, finely chopped

½ green pepper, finely chopped

salt

pepper

PREPARATION:

1. Preheat the oven to 300°F.

2. Combine all the crust ingredients in a bowl and spread the mixture over the entire surface of the beef brisket. Immediately place the flank in the oven to roast for 2½ hours. Increase the temperature to 400°F and cook for another 15 minutes to make sure the coffee crust is extra-crispy.

3. In a bowl, combine all the ingredients for the salsa criolla, except the salt and pepper, making sure to mix well. Season with the salt and pepper to taste and let sit for 15 minutes.

sea

Many people have yet to venture into eating more seafood, be it out of fear or because of a bad experience with seafood in the past, or simply because they think it takes a long time to make. With my selection of recipes I'll show you that seafood is essential for any home chef and can be prepared deliciously without having to spend too much time in the kitchen.

First I want to explain the reasons why we should all be more open to consuming fish and seafood. To start, seafood is very healthy, with lots of proteins, vitamins, and good fats for our bodies. In Spanish we have a saying *"barriguita llena, corazón contento,"* which basically means "full belly, happy heart," and this couldn't be truer than when we eat fish. Fish has a large quantity of polyunsaturated fats, which have been proven to help prevent cardiovascular disease. A healthy heart is also a happy heart.

Additionally, seafood's variety and versatility are of great value in the kitchen, giving the home chef lots of options. Seafood's other advantage is that nowadays you can find it fresh almost anywhere; you can even purchase some varieties on the Internet.

At the beginning of this book, I explained how to choose the freshest seafood at the supermarket (pages 36–37). It's also important to understand how fish and seafood are categorized and the best cooking methods for each. I've also included a few extra tips so you can handle your seafood well. After all, cooking goes beyond a recipe: It's an art and a philosophy with an endless wealth of information!

Types of Fish

Fish can be categorized several ways within the culinary world; there are so many varieties that it's useful to classify them according to some type of order. One way to group them is according to their shape, dividing them into flat and round fish. Another way is by color, which gives us blue and white categories. Finally, some are grouped according to their fat content, which I think is the best method. In this category, fish are divided into three groups: oily, semi-oily, and lean.

- **Oily fish:** These are fish with the highest oil content, up to 10 percent depending on the species. Some fish within this first group are saltwater fish, such as the popular tuna, the sardine (depending on the season), and the swordfish, although there are others that move from salt water to freshwater without a problem, such as the popular salmon and trout. Their high oil content is a feature of their migratory nature; their oil reserve is vital for their long-distance journeys. Another important point regarding these fish is they tend to be a little harder to digest than lean fish. If you have a sensitive stomach, I recommend grilling them to decrease their oil content.

- **Semi-oily fish:** This group is a cross between oily and lean fish. These fish have between 2½ and 6 percent oil. Many oily fish can fall into this category, depending on the time of year, if they lose some of their oil reserve. Some classic semi-oily fish include the golden dorado, the sea bass, and the red sea bream.

- **Lean fish:** Since they don't have to travel long distances in search of food, these fish don't need a large oil reserve. That's why their oil content does not surpass 2½ percent. Most of these species live in the depths of the sea. Some of the most popular ones include cod, hake, and tilapia. Because of their lower oil content, they're usually easier to digest. Likewise, they're incredibly versatile when it comes to cooking, since you can roast, griddle, steam, and even fry them.

seafood

Seafood are incredible creatures with a unique physical structure, but don't let looks fool you! They're just as delicious and nutritious as fish. There's a huge amount of seafood in the world, in different shapes, sizes, and colors, but they are usually divided into two groups: crustaceans and mollusks.

- **Crustaceans:** One of the sea's delicacies! They're known for having a hard shell over their body and, of course, for their delicious meat. This group includes lobsters, crabs, shrimp or prawns, crayfish, and more.

Shrimp and prawns can usually be found year-round. However, some crab and lobster species are available only in certain seasons. You can always find out more about when these species are in season in your region at a trusted supermarket.

When they're raw, crustaceans tend to look quite unappetizing, tinged by an unattractive gray color throughout their bodies. However, a chemical reaction occurs when they're cooked, and they take on a spectacular reddish color, which makes them look scrumptious. If you've purchased frozen crustaceans, make sure they're completely thawed before you cook them so that you'll get their best flavor.

■ **Mollusks:** Mollusks have a shell that protects their soft bodies. Although some think they're hard to eat, these delights from the sea are extremely popular throughout the world. The most commonly consumed mollusks are mussels, oysters, and clams. These species usually live at the bottom of the sea; some adhere to rocks or are buried in the sand. Also, given the great demand, many are grown in marine or fish farms.

the best way to cook fish

When it comes to cooking fish, it's important to decide if you're going to use fillets or a whole fish. To cook an amazing dish without spending too much time in the kitchen, fillets are the way to go. They're easier to handle and the meat cooks in very little time. In fact, many people overcook fillets without realizing it.

Another advantage of fillets is that all you need is a pan, a burner, some oil, and you're ready to go. Fillets can also be grilled, but if you're not used to cooking fish, I recommend you start with a pan. Cooking fish fillets in a pan gives the skin that crispy texture without drying out the rest of the fish.

To help you determine when the fish fillet has reached its ideal cooking point, I have a few easy tips you can use at home. First, the inside of the fish should be around 175°F, which you can monitor with a kitchen thermometer. Just like with beef, some people like their fillets (usually tuna or salmon) somewhat rare in the center. If this is you, or you have a guest who has this preference, I recommend that while you're cooking the fish, you make a few small incisions with a knife to check the center, and remove the fillet when it's reached the desired doneness.

The fish's texture is also a good indicator. The ideal cooked fillet meat should be easy to cut—even applying light pressure on it causes some of the tender, flaky meat

to fall off—and its color should be uniform from its center to its edges. Finally, when you're about to serve it, make sure to place it on the plate incision side down, so that you don't ruin your presentation.

You can also make a succulent whole fish. The bones make the meat more flavorful, juicy, and tender. I also think that serving a whole fish gives a magic touch to the dish's presentation at any table. Just seeing a sea specimen outside its natural habitat, served on a table, decorated with vinaigrettes and dressings, truly creates a unique experience.

Compared to fish fillets, the whole fish takes longer to cook. It's usually done over low heat so that it cooks evenly. It's fairly easy to tell if it's cooked or if it still needs more time. The rule is simple: If the meat is detached from the bone, the fish is ready to eat. If not, don't serve it yet!

A good way to guarantee that a whole fish has wonderful flavor and texture is to cook it in a pan that's close in size to the fish. This will help the fish keep and reabsorb its own juices. The same principle can be applied when you are roasting fish in the oven: Make sure the oven dish is the right size.

Likewise, the seasonings play a major role when making a whole fish. You can dress it with aromatic herbs and lemon slices to enhance its flavor. Some even stuff it, as you would a turkey, with spices and vegetables, so that the meat inside also takes on a delicious flavor.

> You experiment with different varieties of fish and seafood to turn your recipes into unique and special dishes.

the best way to cook seafood

There are so many types of seafood and so many ways to cook them that it would be too much information for this book. So I'm going to concentrate on the most popular and common methods that can be quickly and easily executed at home.

Let's start with the extremely easy—cooking mussels and clams. The best way to make them is in a pot with boiling liquid, which can be anything from plain water, to water aromatized with herbs or onions and shallots, to white wine, to a brine.

Scallops, on the other hand, are cooked differently: You can steam them, cook them in a pan, or even grill them. Some prefer them raw, as I do. I simply add a little salt and lemon and I'm all set. Always make sure to thoroughly wash them before you cook or eat them, and also make sure they're very fresh if you're going to eat them under-cooked or raw.

As for crustaceans such as shrimp and prawns, both are delicious fried, but the most common cooking method is boiling or griddling in a pan. When peeling, make sure to keep the heads and tails! You can use them later to make flavorful broths or sauces (see page 96).

Crabs and lobsters tend to be cooked the same way. The most common method is boiling, and the meat can later be seasoned with butter or lemon. In some parts of Asia, after these crustaceans are boiled, the chef fries the succulent meat. Imagine the delicious result from the combination of flavors and textures!

These fish and seafood cooking tips are just some basic techniques. I recommend that as your confidence in the kitchen grows, you experiment with different varieties of fish and seafood to turn your recipes into unique and special dishes.

Serving a whole fish gives a magic touch to the dish's presentation at any table.

In Spanish we have a saying *"barriguita llena, corazón contento,"* which basically means "full belly, happy heart," and this couldn't be truer than when we eat fish.

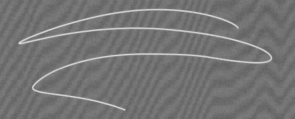

cod *a la* "*vizcaina*"

SERVES 4

I've always enjoyed cod, even as a child, because I loved seeing how it was preserved in salt. This is another recipe from my mentor, Señor David, that, although it is often made in Spain, has a significant Portuguese influence and is said to have come to Spain through the Galician border. Although it takes some time to make this dish, its flavor is unrivaled, making the wait 100 percent worth it.

INGREDIENTS:

1 pound salt cod, cut into 4 even pieces

4 potatoes, cubed

2 onions, chopped

4 hard-boiled eggs, sliced

½ cup green olives, pitted

3 cloves garlic

2 tablespoons capers

1 red pepper, diced

4 tomatoes, diced

1 8-ounce can crushed tomatoes

1 cup white wine

¼ cup olive oil

1 cup water

2 bay leaves

white rice, cooked, as side dish

PREPARATION:

1. Remove the salt by placing the fish in a bowl with cold water. Change the water every 2 hours, at least 4 times.

2. In a large pot, combine the potatoes, cod, onions, eggs, olives, garlic, capers, red pepper, diced tomatoes, and crushed tomatoes.

3. Add the white wine, olive oil, water, and bay leaves. Bring the mixture to a boil, lower the heat to medium, and cook for 30 minutes covered.

4. Serve with a side of white rice.

clams with white beans and chorizo

SERVES 4

Finesse! *¡Finura!* Elegance! This is a word we usually associate with expensive food, but not in this case. Don't let the long list of ingredients intimidate you. This recipe is very easy to make. I recommend you make this dish over the weekend to share with your family. Double the ingredients if you are expecting more than 4 people. If you want to accompany it with wine, I recommend white.

INGREDIENTS:

olive oil

1 onion, finely chopped

4 cloves garlic, minced

1 carrot, diced

2 stalks celery, chopped

2 dried Spanish chorizos, chopped

4 bay leaves

2 15-ounce cans white beans, drained

2 cups vegetable broth

FOR THE CLAMS

olive oil

1 shallot, finely chopped

6 cloves garlic, minced

2 tablespoons chopped parsley, plus extra for garnish

½ teaspoon red pepper flakes

2 dozen clams

½ bottle white wine

PREPARATION:

1. In a large pot over medium-high heat, add a drizzle of olive oil and sauté the onion, garlic, carrot, celery, and chorizo. Add the bay leaves, white beans, and vegetable broth, and cook for 1 hour.

2. Meanwhile, prepare the clams. In a medium saucepot, heat a drizzle of olive oil and sauté for 5 minutes the shallot with the garlic, parsley, and red pepper. Add the clams and cook for 1 minute, increase the heat to high, and add the white wine. Bring to a boil and turn off the heat.

main dishes

205

3. Pour the clams into the pot of white beans and chorizo and cook for a few more minutes.

4. Serve garnished with finely chopped parsley.

chef james tip >> To fully rinse out any sand in the clams, immerse them in a bowl of water and add salt and 2 teaspoons of white vinegar. Let the clams sit for several minutes and they will naturally release any sand deposits. Once they are rinsed, they're ready to use.

fish *a la veracruzana*

SERVES 4

Travel around the world from your kitchen with this classic recipe from Veracruz, Mexico. This is one of the star recipes at my restaurant, Sabores by Chef James. Incredibly simple to make, this dish owes its amazing presentation to the intense color of the Veracruz sauce that dresses the fish. With its delightful aroma and flavor, this dish will certainly become a favorite!

INGREDIENTS:

olive oil

1 onion, chopped

4 cloves garlic, minced

2 pounds tomatoes, diced

1 cup water

3 bay leaves

1 tablespoon oregano

½ cup green olives

2 tablespoons capers

4 guajillo chiles, finely chopped

4 medium-size whitefish fillets,
   seasoned with salt and pepper

parsley

PREPARATION:

1. In a pan over medium-high heat, add a splash of oil and sauté the onions and garlic for 3 minutes or until the onions are translucent.

2. In a baking tray, place the tomatoes in the broiler and cook until the skins are black. Take out the tomatoes from the broiler.

3. Add the broiled tomatoes, the water, bay leaves, oregano, olives, capers, and chiles to the pan and cook for 30 minutes over low heat uncovered.

4. Once the sauce is ready, in a separate pan over medium-high heat, cook the fish fillets until the meat is opaque.

5. Top with the sauce and garnish with parsley and olive oil.

chef james tip >> Burned tomatoes make all the difference here. Broil them until their skin turns black.

shrimp and fish moqueca

SERVES 4

Amazing flavor and texture—that's how I describe this seafood recipe. The *moqueca* is a typical Brazilian dish, a type of coconut-based broth, aromatized with vegetables, that is used to cook the shrimp and fish. Preparing this dish is the only thing that will take some time, because the actual cooking is quite fast. Come on, go for it!

INGREDIENTS:

   1 yellow onion, diced

   1 tomato, chopped

   3 cloves garlic, crushed

   5 tablespoons cilantro, plus more, chopped, for garnish

   juice of half of a lemon

   salt

   1 pound red snapper, cut into 1½-inch cubes

   ½ pound shrimp

   ¼ cup olive oil

   1 yellow onion, julienned

   1 red pepper, chopped

   1 green pepper, chopped

   1 yellow pepper, chopped

   1 cup coconut milk

   1 tomato, sliced in rounds

PREPARATION:

1. In a blender, mix the diced onion, tomato, 1½ of the garlic cloves, 5 tablespoons of cilantro, lemon juice, and salt until the mixture is well processed.

2. In a glass bowl, combine the snapper and shrimp and add the blended vegetables. Cover the bowl with plastic wrap and let the mixture sit in the refrigerator for 1 hour.

3. In a pan over medium heat, add the olive oil and sauté the julienned onions for 3 to 4 minutes. Add the remaining 1½ garlic cloves and the peppers, and sauté for 3 min-

main dishes

utes. Add the fish-shrimp-vegetable mixture, then the coconut milk. Bring to a boil and add the tomato slices over it. Cover and cook for 10 minutes over medium heat.

4. Garnish with cilantro. Serve, preferably with rice.

chef james tip >> Avoid dicing the fish in cubes that are too small because the dish will need less cooking time and it will affect your recipe's outcome—1½-inch cubes are a good size for this recipe.

Seafood is very healthy, with lots of proteins, vitamins, and good fats for our bodies.

stewed fish with chorizo

SERVES 4

This dish is perfect for a weekend lunch with the family. The flavor and the chorizo's oil go wonderfully well with the tender texture of the fish, which cooks quickly, since it's diced, saving you time in the kitchen. The cumin and smoked paprika play an important role, noticeable at the first bite. The dish is also incredibly aromatic—the key to which is the sautéed ingredients, or as we say in Spanish, the *sofrito*. This creates the recipe's flavorful foundation.

INGREDIENTS:

2 Spanish chorizos, cut in ½-inch slices

2 cloves garlic, minced

1 red pepper, chopped

1 teaspoon cumin

1 teaspoon smoked paprika

4 ounces crushed tomatoes

8 ounces tomatoes in sauce

2 sprigs thyme

1 pound whitefish, diced into 1½-inch cubes

1 tablespoon cilantro, finely chopped

1 lemon, cut into fourths

PREPARATION:

1. In a large pot over medium-high heat, cook the chorizo. Once it starts releasing some of its oil, add the garlic, red pepper, cumin, and paprika. Add the crushed tomatoes and cook for 5 minutes.

2. Add the tomatoes in sauce and the thyme and cook for another 4 minutes.

3. Add the fish, turn off the heat, and let the dish sit for 5 minutes.

4. Garnish with cilantro and squeezed lemon, and serve.

hawaiian fish tacos

SERVES 6 TO 8

During one of my trips to Mexico, I heard someone say, "Everything tastes better inside a tortilla." I couldn't agree more, especially when it comes to this recipe. At the first bite, you will taste the delicate balance of flavors—the fish's freshness, the lemon's acidity, and the orange's and pineapple's sweetness and sourness. This is another recipe that will break the kitchen monotony, and since it's fast and easy to make, you can prepare it whenever you feel like it. *¡Óraleee!*

INGREDIENTS:

4 fillets tilapia

juice of 1 orange

juice of 1 lemon

2 tablespoons honey

1 cup cilantro, chopped (leave some to garnish)

¼ cup vegetable oil

4 corn tortillas

FOR THE PINEAPPLE SALSA

½ whole pineapple, peeled and cut in slices

3 tablespoons olive oil

½ onion, grilled and then diced

1 orange pepper, grilled and then diced

juice of 1 orange

juice of 1 lemon

salt

pepper

1 jalapeño, chopped, for garnish

PREPARATION:

1. In a Ziploc bag, marinate the tilapia fillets with the orange juice, lemon, honey, cilantro, and oil. Keep inside the refrigerator for 1 hour.

2. In an oiled pan, cook the fish over high heat for 3 minutes on each side. Then, remove from the heat.

3. To make the salsa, coat the pineapple with olive oil and place it on a well-heated grill, brown for 3 minutes on each side, and remove. Repeat the process with the onion and orange pepper. Finely chop the pineapple, pepper, and onion, and place them in a bowl, followed by the orange juice, lemon juice, the remaining olive oil, salt, and pepper.

4. Lightly heat a tortilla, add a fish fillet, and top it off with the grilled pineapple salsa. Serve with the jalapeño as garnish. Repeat with the remaining tortillas and fish.

shrimp *a la diabla*

SERVES 4

There are few recipes where shrimp has as much flavor as in this one. The name came about one day when, while I was sitting with my production team, we were told that the cast of the famous Telemundo telenovela *Santa diabla* was coming to our show. The guests were Carlos Ponce and Gaby Espino. That's when, as fast as a bolt of lightning, we invented this delicious and slightly hot recipe. I love it, but if you're not a fan of spicy food, you can forego the habanero chiles.

INGREDIENTS:

olive oil

4 cloves garlic, minced

1 red pepper, chopped

½ onion, chopped

½ cup white wine

4 chipotle chiles with adobo

12 ounces crushed tomatoes

2 habanero chiles

1 tablespoon Worcestershire sauce

4 tablespoons tomato sauce

3 pounds shrimp

1 cup cooked white rice

parsley, chopped, for garnish

PREPARATION:

1. In a large pot, add a drizzle of olive oil and sauté over medium heat the garlic, red pepper, and onion for 4 to 5 minutes. Once they are lightly browned, add the white wine and reduce by ¾. Add the chipotle chiles, tomatoes, habanero chiles, Worcestershire sauce, and tomato sauce. Cook for 30 minutes over medium heat uncovered. Add the shrimp and cook for another 5 minutes.

2. Serve with rice and garnish with parsley.

grilled whole fish with green salsa

SERVES 4

This dish will quickly become one of your favorites at home. The grilled fish, because it's cooked whole, holds abundant flavor and will win over even your harshest critic. The green salsa gives the dish a very fresh combination of flavors, with the trout acting as a canvas that highlights the wild flavor of the cilantro. This is a dish that will impress.

INGREDIENTS:

1 whole trout

olive oil

salt

pepper

FOR THE SALSA VERDE

8 tomatillos, grilled

2 serrano chiles, grilled

1 clove garlic

1 onion

½ cup water

1 cup cilantro, plus extra for garnish

juice of 1 lemon

PREPARATION:

1. Preheat a grill or preheat the oven to 400°F. Season the fish with olive oil, salt, and pepper. Place on the grill or in the oven and cook for 8 minutes on each side. Transfer the whole fish to a serving platter.

2. In a blender, mix all the salsa verde ingredients for 1 minute.

3. To serve, cover the fish with the salsa verde and garnish with cilantro.

chef james tip >>

I recommend that you use fresh fish for this recipe. Remember that a good way to check its freshness is by lightly pressing the fish with your finger. If it bounces back to its original shape, it's fresh.

sea bass with brown sugar glaze

SERVES 2

You're only 20 minutes away from savoring this wonder in the kitchen! I always say that the freedom to satisfy our palates and implement creativity prevails in the kitchen, and that's the case with this recipe—combining fish with sugar. (Though it might sound strange, the combination is not too far from sweet and sour chicken.) The sea bass is a flavorful fish that goes very well with sweet glazes. I tried to give this recipe a healthy touch, which is why I recommend you use brown sugar. A final tip is to use the oven when cooking to ensure that the delicious juices are sealed in the fish.

INGREDIENTS:

2 tablespoons Dijon mustard

¼ cup brown sugar

2 fillets sea bass

½ pound sweet peas

2 tablespoons olive oil

¼ cup sliced almonds

salt

pepper

PREPARATION:

1. Preheat the oven to 450°F.

2. Put the sea bass in a baking dish and leave it in the oven for 12 to 15 minutes and then remove the fish from the oven.

3. In a bowl, mix the mustard with the sugar to form a paste.

4. Spread the paste on top of the sea bass.

5. In a large pot, boil enough water to cover the peas. Add the peas and cook for 1 minute. Remove the peas from the water.

6. In a pan over medium heat, add olive oil and sauté the almonds with the peas for 2 minutes. Season with salt and pepper, and serve with the sea bass.

cod with cilantro, cream, peas, bacon, and sherry

SERVES 4

Cod is a very versatile fish, and in this recipe it is truly marvelous. The succulent sherry bacon in the bed of peas pairs beautifully with the flaky, tender cod, and the cilantro sauce adds a creamy texture. You can prepare this dish very quickly since cod is easy to cook—so you'll have more time to relax and enjoy your meal!

INGREDIENTS:

FOR THE BACON, PEAS, AND SHERRY

6 slices bacon, chopped

½ yellow onion, finely chopped

1 cup peas

¼ cup sherry

FOR THE COD

1 tablespoon butter

1 tablespoon flour

1 cup whole milk

salt

2 tablespoons cream

1 pound fresh cod fillets

½ cup cilantro, finely chopped

PREPARATION:

1. In a pan over medium-high heat, sauté the bacon until it's crunchy. Add the onion and cook for 3 minutes. Add the peas and cook for 2 minutes. Add the sherry and reduce by ¾.

2. In a large pan over medium-high heat, melt the butter. Add the flour, making sure it dissolves well. Slowly add the milk so that it thickens, and cook for 1 minute. Season with salt and add the cream. Reduce until the mixture coats the back of a spoon. Add the cod and cook for 8 minutes. Add the cilantro and remove from the heat.

3. Arrange the mixture of sherry, bacon, and peas on individual plates, and top with the cod and cream sauce.

salmon *a la vinaigrette*

This recipe is proof that you can enjoy a wonderful meal without spending too much time in the kitchen. Salmon is spectacular when prepared in a pan, and the vinaigrette adds a touch of freshness to each bite. When I'm counting calories, I make steamed veggies to accompany the fish, but rice makes a magnificent side dish too. It's the perfect dish to prepare when you want something good and quick.

INGREDIENTS:

- 2 fillets salmon
- salt
- pepper
- ½ cup ketchup
- 1 chayote, finely chopped
- ¼ teaspoon chives, chopped
- ¼ cup parsley, finely chopped
- ½ cup olive oil
- 2 teaspoons Worcestershire sauce
- 2 tablespoons hot sauce

PREPARATION:

1. Season the salmon fillets with salt and pepper.

2. In a pan over high heat, cook the salmon for 3 to 4 minutes on each side.

3. While the fish is cooking, mix the rest of the ingredients in a bowl and beat well with a fork until they're well incorporated.

4. Remove the salmon from the pan and serve topped with a couple of tablespoons of the vinaigrette.

pasta and rice

Pasta and rice are some of the ingredients I love the most, given their tendency to bring families together and because they bring back wonderful memories of my own family. Think about it: We often gather to eat paella or to share a delicious pasta, hence the classic term *"la pasta de la abuela"* or "grandmother's pasta." These dishes, often containing well-known traditional ingredients, have found their way into Latin American cuisines by way of European immigrants. These foods, and the cultural tendency associated with them, of bringing together many loved ones—well, to me that equals happiness.

I believe one of the reasons pasta and rice dishes are so popular is that they go a long way. They are incredibly affordable and can feed many. I remember those endless pots of rice at home! Both are also very easy to make, which is convenient when having to cook for many without much time to spare.

We also can't forget the cultural significance of ingredients, namely, in Spain and Italy. Paella is arguably Spain's national dish, and pasta is part of Italy's great heritage and legacy. It's no wonder that European immigration to South America has really merged the two cultures, and with this, what and how we eat.

Given the great variety of rice and pasta, the possibilities are endless. But before you start preparing these delicious recipes, I want to share more about these magical ingredients. As a chef, I always want you to learn things you didn't know before, to make you feel excited about being able to prepare your own dishes with these ingredients, and to help you set your goal to satisfy everyone's palate at home.

pasta

Pastas are made with nothing other than water and flour. However, within this simple formula, there are variations, such as the type of flour used and the combinations with water used to make them. For example, the family of my dear friend Mauro Scattolini made their own pasta with flour, water, and egg. It was a huge family affair that lasted from the morning, when they would start making the pasta, to the evening, when they all sat down to enjoy it. It was truly exquisite. What I loved the most was how the food was served. As we sat around the table, they'd pour all the pasta (sauce and all!) straight onto the table. That's how it was traditionally served, which to this day I thoroughly enjoy. They called this pasta *sopra la tavola* and the younger ones had the hardest task of all: cleaning up the table!

I won't get into how to make homemade pasta because it does take time, and my goal with this book is to make your kitchen experience more convenient and easier. Besides, you don't need to make pasta from scratch in order to make a spectacular dish. Nowadays you can also find good-quality, flavorful pasta sauce at most supermarkets. When choosing, check the label to make sure it's made from only the best ingredients to ensure you're getting a quality sauce that's the next best thing to homemade.

> Nowadays you can also find good-quality, flavorful pasta sauce at most supermarkets.

One of the things I like the most about pastas and their varieties is that they're endless: from classic spaghetti and fabulous cannelloni to my favorite: pappardelle. We can divide the pasta world into three groups: short, long, and stuffed pastas.

- Short pastas, such as penne and elbow, are usually used with thick sauces that have big chunks of vegetables or meat, or with a seafood sauce. The short size of these pastas makes it easier to eat these dishes since they're already loaded with sauce. However, this doesn't mean that you'll never find a chunky sauce over a bed of long pasta or that you have to run to the supermarket to buy short pasta because the long one that you already have in your pantry won't do. It's just something to keep in mind when choosing your pasta.

- Long pastas, such as spaghetti and noodles, tend to be served with light tomato sauces, oils, and smooth cream sauces. Here the rule is: The thicker the noodle, the more sauce will attach to it, and the better the flavor of each bite. You should also keep in mind that the thicker the noodle, the longer it will take to cook al dente.

- When it comes to stuffed pastas, the sauce helps enhance the filling's flavor. Usually, stuffed pastas are served with meat juice, or a sauce that includes the flavors of what's inside the pasta. The most popular ones in this group include ravioli, cappelletti, and sorrentini. These kinds of pasta are amazing because each bite of pasta with sauce carries an explosion of flavor.

how to make pasta al dente

We've all heard that the best pasta is cooked al dente. There's nothing worse than an overcooked pasta that feels "rubbery." "Al dente" means "to the tooth," and it refers to when pasta is cooked firm to the bite.

To obtain this ideal texture, you must know exactly how much water you'll need to cook the pasta. Generally, use 1 quart of water for every ¼ pound of pasta. If you use too little water, you risk the pasta coming out sticky, which happens because noodles release starch while cooking, and if there isn't enough water to dissolve it, the starch readheres to the pasta. If you don't have a pot large enough for the recommended amount of water, you can add a splash of oil to the water. The starch adheres to the oil so it doesn't end up on the pasta again.

Once you've calculated the amount of water, bring it to a boil. Once it's boiling, add 1 tablespoon of salt for each quart of water in the pot. This is mainly done so that the pasta absorbs some of the salt and acquires more flavor for the final result. Then add the pasta and cover the pot. When the water begins to boil again, uncover the pot and stir the pasta, and continue stirring every 2 minutes until the cooking time indicated on the package is complete.

To test the pasta, bite into it and see if it's resistant to the teeth or cut a piece and check the center. If the center is lighter than the outside, the pasta is not yet ready. If your recipe calls for you to bake the pasta, stop cooking it and strain it before it reaches al dente, to allow it to finish cooking in the oven.

When the pasta is ready, quickly strain out the water and serve immediately. Instead of mixing all of the sauce and pasta together in one serving bowl, I recommend that you serve the pasta and sauce in individual portions. This way, you can store the leftover pasta and sauce separately. Although, at least in my family, there are usually no leftovers!

rice

Everyone loves rice! I bet you didn't know it's the second most produced grain after corn. Incredible, right? Currently, there are more than 90,000 wild rice samples in the International Rice Genebank. This means that we could basically try a different type of wild rice every day for the next 245 years and we still won't have tried them all. That's how diverse this incredible grain is!

In Latin American and many other cuisines, rice is the quintessential side dish, valued for the way its light flavor combines with meats, seafood, fish, sauces, and vegetables. We like it so much, in fact, that some genius even turned it into a dessert, creating the famous rice pudding.

In Asian cuisine, rice is an essential part of a dish and considered more than just a side. For example, in Japan, when it comes to sushi, rice is just as important as the fish, if not more so, and rice is the ingredient used to make sake. In China it is use in a great variety of dishes, such as fried rice and its infinite varieties; and in India, rice is vital in dishes such as biryani, rice mixed with spices and meat or vegetables. In Italy, rice is also a very popular main ingredient, namely, in the exquisite risottos.

I always joke around and say that the different types of rice have different personalities. Some require longer cooking time and are hard; I call this type grumpy rice. There are others that are easier to cook, which I call gentle grains. However, the world actually divides this ingredient into long-grain rice, medium-grain rice, and short-grain rice. As the names suggest, they're basically differentiated by grain size, and the different sizes are used for different recipes.

- Long-grain rice contains high amounts of amylose, a type of starch, and that's why it needs to be cooked in a considerable amount of water and, obviously, over a longer period of time than the shorter varieties. This is one of the most-used grains in Chinese and Indian cuisine. Once cooked, it's firm and loose.

- Medium-grain rice, also known as bomba rice, is used in Spanish cuisine and is the quintessential choice for the delicious paellas. It's also used throughout Latin America. Given its shape and features, it can also be used to make risotto, although the traditional grains used in Italy for this dish are usually carnaroli or arborio rice.

- Short-grain rice is usually found in Japan, northern China, and Korea. Given its round shape and ability to stick together, this variety of rice is ideal for making sushi. This is also the rice used to make the delicious rice pudding, so I'm sure this type of grain has already won over most of your hearts.

There are more than 90,000 wild rice samples in the International Rice Genebank.

the best way to cook rice

Although it's easy to make, sometimes rice doesn't come out as planned. This is primarily due to some mistake made while preparing it. You can't be bad at making rice! But mistakes happen to everyone, and that's why I've included some quick tips that will help you make perfectly cooked, fluffy rice.

- Make sure you cook rice in a pot that's in good condition. Oftentimes, people ignore this small detail and the rice ends up sticking to the bottom of the pot.

- The water-to-rice ratio is a simple but major detail that can mean the difference between loose rice and pasty rice. The amount of water you use will vary with the type of rice you're cooking. For white rice, the typical ratio is 2 cups of water for every cup of rice. For brown rice, use 2½ cups of water for every cup of rice.

main dishes

■ Once you've rinsed the rice, put it in a pot with a splash of olive oil and, if you like, a garlic clove over medium-high heat. Stir well until every grain is coated in oil. Add the water.

■ Keep an eye on your rice pot, because it's important to notice when the water reaches a boil. When this happens, reduce the heat and continue cooking over low heat for 20 minutes, covered. If you don't lower the heat, you risk having the water evaporate and the rice stick to the pot.

If you follow these four simple steps, you will have excellent rice. Now you can venture into preparing the following delicious recipes. Roll up your sleeves and get ready to cook!

One of the reasons
pasta and rice dishes
are so popular is that
they go a long way.

linguine with chipotle-marinara sauce

SERVES 4 TO 6

This recipe gives a unique touch to pasta by adding some chipotle to a classic marinara sauce. The chipotle adds a smoky and lightly spicy tone, and the result is exquisite!

INGREDIENTS:

1 pound linguine

olive oil

1 onion, chopped

4 cloves garlic, minced

2 stalks celery, chopped

2 carrots, finely chopped

32 ounces roasted crushed tomatoes

2 bay leaves

salt

pepper

4 tablespoons chipotle paste

fresh oregano, for garnish

PREPARATION:

1. Cook the linguine according to the instructions on the package.

2. Meanwhile, in a deep pot over medium-high heat, pour a splash of oil and sauté the onion, garlic, celery, and carrots until they're soft, usually around 7 minutes. Add the tomatoes and bay leaves, season with salt and pepper, and add the chipotle paste. Cook uncovered over low heat and stir for 1 hour.

3. Serve with the linguine, garnishing with fresh oregano leaves.

chef james tip >> How much salt should you add to the water when cooking pasta? Enough for the water to taste like seawater.

pasta with cilantro pesto

SERVES 4

Sauces must always enhance the flavor of the dishes they are created for; they must never overshadow it. This pasta with cilantro pesto perfectly achieves this goal, and because cilantro is very aromatic, it's the perfect replacement for basil in pesto. This recipe is ideal for lunch, when you don't have too much time to cook. It came about when I was creating the brunch menu for Sabores by Chef James, my Miami restaurant, where I wanted to make a pasta with pesto, but with ingredients used in Latin cuisines.

INGREDIENTS:

2 cups cilantro

½ cup olive oil

⅓ cup pepitas tostadas (pumpkin seeds)

½ cup Cotija cheese, crumbled

juice of 2 lemons

2 cloves garlic

1 pound penne pasta

PREPARATION:

1. In a blender, combine the cilantro, olive oil, pepitas, cheese, lemon juice, and garlic. Blend until the mixture is uniform and creamy.

2. Cook the pasta following the package instructions.

3. Scoop 4 tablespoons of pesto into a large bowl and add the pasta straight from the pot. Mix well and serve.

lasagna enchilada

SERVES 4 TO 6

I guarantee this recipe will make everyone's jaw drop! If you like traditional lasagna and you like tacos, then you'll love this Mexican fusion dish. I came up with this recipe while participating in a cooking contest in which I had to pick two pieces of paper from two different bowls: One bowl had the names of countries and the other had typical dishes from those countries. Whatever combination I randomly picked was the dish I had to make. I got Mexico and lasagna. The dish ended up being so good that I decided to include it here and share it with you. I love it because it has a homemade touch; eating it makes me feel good, and the spiciness makes you feel alive.

INGREDIENTS:

2 tablespoons olive oil

20 corn tortillas

1 pound shredded chicken

4 poblano chiles, roasted whole

1 pound Mexican queso fresco, grated

2 cups Mexican cream

1 cup cilantro, chopped

2 red onions, chopped

3 tomatoes, diced

1 tablespoon cumin

PREPARATION:

1. Preheat the oven to 400°F.

2. Grease a baking dish with the olive oil. Cover the bottom of the dish with tortillas, prepping to create layers with the different ingredients.

3. Chop the poblano chiles. Then layer the chicken, then poblano chiles, queso fresco, cream, cilantro, onion, tomatoes, and cumin, followed by another layer of tortillas. Repeat until you've filled the dish to the top. Finish with any leftover cheese.

4. Bake uncovered for 25 minutes and then serve.

main dishes

241

chorizo rice

SERVES 4 TO 6

This dish is a great alternative to serve at family gatherings because, like with all rice dishes, you can make plenty of food without putting in too much effort. Also, the chorizo's great flavor seasons the rice, giving it a smoky taste that everyone will love. Let's get to work!

INGREDIENTS:

4 spicy chorizos

olive oil

1 red onion, julienned

4 cloves garlic, minced

1 red pepper, julienned

1 tablespoon smoked paprika

1 cup rice

¼ cup sherry

2 cups chicken broth

parsley, finely chopped, for garnish

PREPARATION:

1. With a knife, make a fine incision on the chorizos' surface and remove the filling. Discard the casing.

2. In a deep pot, add a drizzle of olive oil, followed by the chorizo meat. Brown over high heat. Remove the chorizo from the pot.

3. Using the same pot, combine the onion, garlic, and pepper, and sauté over medium heat for about 4 minutes. Add the paprika and cook for another minute. Return the chorizo to the pot, add the rice, and lightly toast with the rest of the ingredients.

4. Add the sherry and use a wooden spoon to loosen the bits that are stuck to the bottom of the pot. Add the chicken broth. Cook following the rice instructions.

5. Sprinkle with parsley and serve.

wild rice with mushrooms

When we talk about rice, especially in Latin America, we tend to think about the classic white rice. But there are so many rice varieties around the world, and one of the most common is wild rice. The distinctive color and great complexity of flavors make this rice a fascinating ingredient. I first tried it at culinary school, and I was captivated by its texture and nutty notes, which bring to mind walnuts and hazelnuts. For this recipe, I mix the rice with mushrooms, which perfectly complement the rice's complex flavor. I hope you try it!

INGREDIENTS:

- 1 cup wild rice
- 2 tablespoons butter
- ½ onion, chopped
- ½ pound mixed mushrooms, chopped
- ¼ cup Marsala
- 4 tablespoons dried cranberries
- parsley, finely chopped, for garnish
- 1 tablespoon olive oil

PREPARATION:

1. Cook the rice following the package instructions.

2. In a pan, melt the butter over medium-high heat and sauté the onion. When the onion is transparent (about 3 to 4 minutes), add the mushrooms and cook for 3 minutes. Add the Marsala and reduce by ¼.

3. Add the cooked rice, followed by the cranberries, parsley, and olive oil, stir well to incorporate, and serve.

chef james tip >> This dish is quintessentially vegetarian, but if you'd like to add some protein, I recommend adding 1 chicken breast, cubed.

main dishes

chaufa rice with chicken

SERVES 4 TO 6

This incredible recipe comes from the great combination of Asian and Latin American cuisines. A perfect example of fast cooking, this dish is very easy to make, and it's also a delicious way to use leftovers. In short, it's a recipe that will make anyone smile.

INGREDIENTS:

olive oil

8 ounces chicken, diced

1 egg

¼ cup scallions, finely chopped

1 teaspoon garlic, minced

¼ red pepper, finely chopped

1 teaspoon minced ginger

1 cup day-old cooked rice

2 tablespoons soy sauce

3 tablespoons sesame oil

PREPARATION:

1. In a very hot pan, drizzle sesame oil and add the diced chicken. Cook for 4 to 5 minutes and then remove the chicken from the pan.

2. In the same pan, scramble the egg and remove from the pan.

3. Also in the same pan, combine the scallions, garlic, pepper, and ginger, and cook over medium heat for 2 minutes. Add the chicken, the rice, and the soy sauce, stir to combine, and cook over high heat for 30 seconds.

4. Return the egg to the pan, add the sesame oil, stir to incorporate, and serve.

seafood paella

SERVES 6

I could describe this dish as a work of art, a masterpiece; picturesque, colorful, striking, and artistic. With seafood decorating the vegetables and infusing the rice with flavor, paella is very poetic. I'm giving you this passionate description because I know how intimidating this recipe might appear, but if you follow the steps, it will turn out great. And once you try it and see how easy to make and delicious it is, you won't even think about going to a restaurant the next time you're craving paella.

INGREDIENTS:

olive oil

1 onion, chopped

4 cloves garlic, minced

1 red pepper, chopped

1 tablespoon smoked paprika

1 pound Valencia rice

1 cup white wine

salt

pepper

2 quarts chicken or shrimp broth

½ pound whitefish

½ pound shrimp

15 mussels

½ pound squid

1 pinch saffron (optional)

olive oil, for garnish

parsley, for garnish

1 lemon, for garnish

PREPARATION:

1. In a large pan over medium-high heat, add a drizzle of olive oil, followed by the onion, garlic, and pepper, and cook for 3 minutes. Add the paprika and cook for another minute.

2. Add the rice and mix until the grains are coated with the oil. Add the white wine and reduce by ¾.

3. Once the wine has reduced, season with the salt and pepper and add the chicken broth. Let the mixture cook over medium-low heat until the liquid has evaporated and the rice is tender, usually around 16 minutes. Turn the heat off, and add the fish, seafood, and saffron (if using). Cover once again and, 5 minutes later, stir well. Finish with olive oil, parsley, and lemon.

chef james tip >> Although many people like stirring the paella while it's cooking, I recommend leaving it alone throughout the cooking process to prevent the rice from releasing extra starch, which can give the paella a gelatinous texture. Furthermore, not stirring the paella guarantees that you'll get that crunchy rice crust at the bottom of the pan, known in Spanish as the *pegao*, that makes this dish so popular.

sweet potato gnocchi

SERVES 4 TO 6

Few things are as satisfying as making your own gnocchi. This recipe is a healthier variation on the usual, and the sweet potato gives the dish a different twist. I promise it will be amazingly flavorful and everyone at home will love it.

INGREDIENTS:

- 1 cup sweet potato puree
- 1 cup ricotta
- 2 eggs
- ½ cup Parmesan cheese, grated, plus extra to finish the dish
- 2 cups flour
- 6 tablespoons butter
- 1 pound mushrooms, sliced
- 3 sprigs thyme
- 2 sprigs rosemary
- 2 cloves garlic, minced
- ¼ cup balsamic vinegar

PREPARATION:

1. In a bowl, combine the sweet potato puree, ricotta, eggs, and Parmesan cheese, and incorporate well until doughy. Add 1½ cups of the flour so that the dough is very sticky. Continue kneading until the dough is soft and less sticky. Shape the dough into a ball. On a clean, flat surface, spread the remaining ½ cup flour, divide the dough into 8 same-size pieces, and shape each one into a 15-inch-long and 1-inch-thick rope. Cut each dough rope into 1-inch pieces and lightly press the flat side of a fork's tines into the gnocchi surface.

2. Bring a large pot filled with ¾ of water to a boil and cook the gnocchi until they rise to the surface and float. Strain.

3. To make the sauce, melt the butter in a pan over high heat. Add the mushrooms, thyme, rosemary, garlic, and balsamic vinegar, and reduce until the mushrooms are covered with a glaze. Add the gnocchi to the pan and mix with the mushrooms and sauce.

4. Serve, finished with Parmesan cheese.

sénia rice with eel and cherry base

Before ending this main dish section, I leave you with something extra-special. I've devoted this book to easy, fast, and, above all, convenient recipes, but I don't want to miss this opportunity to share what could open up for you a totally different world: sophisticated and elaborate cooking at the vanguard of the culinary world that also highlights simplicity and respect for ingredients. As a fan of rice, I wanted to include a recipe shared by a good friend and chef whom I respect and admire: Quique Dacosta. His restaurant Quique Dacosta, in Dénia, Spain, has been awarded with three Michelin stars, the most prestigious recognition in the culinary world. For the adventurous reader who is willing to go for more, this is the challenge for you. When you make it, don't forget to share it with us through your social network, mentioning @chefjames and @qiqedacosta.

FOR THE SMOKED EEL BASE

INGREDIENTS:

- 13 ounces smoked eel
- 1 tablespoon olive oil, for frying
- 12 ounces fresh eel
- 1 clove garlic, purple, unpeeled
- 1 ounce olive oil
- 3½ ounces tender onion, chopped
- 3 ounces carrots, chopped
- 3 ounces leek (the white part), chopped
- 1½ ounces aloin-free aloe vera flesh (five years old), chopped
- 6 black peppercorns
- 10½ monkfish skin
- 12 ounces dried chickpeas, soaked
- 1¾ gallons mineral water
- 4 sprigs Montgó wild rosemary
- 1 tablespoon salt

PREPARATION:

1. Chop and fry the smoked eel in plenty of olive oil. Uniformly brown it and drain well on paper towels.

2. Eviscerate, bleed, and chop the fresh eel. Fry it in the same oil used for the smoked eel, and drain well on paper towels. Reserve the oil.

3. Lightly brown the garlic in a saucepan with 1 ounce of olive oil. Add the chopped vegetables and aloe vera. Let them get some color and add the peppercorns, the monkfish skin, the fried eel, and the soaked chickpeas. Cover with mineral water and bring to a boil. Cook over low heat, without it reaching a boil, for 6 hours. Add the rosemary for it to infuse. Immediately set it aside and let it sit for another 6 hours and drain. Add more salt if necessary.

FOR THE ROSEMARY OLIVE OIL

INGREDIENTS:

½ **gallon light virgin olive oil**

1 **quart grape-seed oil**

10½ **ounces wild Montgó rosemary**

PREPARATION:

Infuse the ingredients in an airtight container at 176°F for 1 hour. Let sit for 6 hours at a cold temperature. Drain and store.

FOR THE CHERRY GARNISH

INGREDIENTS:

2 **pounds Picota cherry pulp**

17 **ounces mineral water**

1 **ounce sugar**

½ **ounce aloe vera powder**

1 **tablespoon rosemary olive oil**

PREPARATION:

1. Decant the cherry pulp and strain it through a cheesecloth. Save the pulp and mix it with water. Let sit for 2 hours, decant, and drain.

2. This makes about 4 cups of clean cherry pulp. Take half of this liquid, add the sugar and aloe powder, and bring to a boil. Remove from the heat and add the other half of the clean cherry pulp.

3. Pour the warm liquid into a syringe and let a few drops fall on the cold rosemary oil. Let cool and coagulate for 12 minutes. Drain and store.

FOR THE RICE
(THE ONION, THE CUTTLEFISH, AND THE RICE'S 2 COOKING PHASES)

(a) Onion Noisette

INGREDIENTS:

> 3½ ounces butter noisette
> 3½ ounces tender onion

PREPARATION:

1. Place the butter in a wide metal container and, once hot, add the chopped onion. Poach it for 3 hours, until it's tender and has a uniformly brown color.

2. While it's still hot, drain it and recover all the butter. This way the onion will have a special flavor without the fat.

(b) The Cuttlefish

INGREDIENTS:

> 17½ ounces fresh Mediterranean cuttlefish

PREPARATION:

Eviscerate and clean the cuttlefish. Dice and set aside.

(c) Cooking the Rice: Phase 1

INGREDIENTS:

> 1 tablespoon of the oil used to fry the smoked eel
> 2 ounces onion noisette
> 9 ounces Sénia rice with D.O. Valencia
> 1¾ pounds smoked eel broth

PREPARATION:

1. Sauté the onion noisette in the smoked eel oil. Add the rice, immediately followed by the hot broth. It's important to not sauté the rice to avoid making the grain waterproof. This way it will easily absorb the rest of the ingredient flavors.

2. When it reaches its first boiling point, lower the heat and cook for 8 minutes.

3. Stop cooking, drain the mix, and cool the rice. Keep the broth for phase 2.

(d) Cooking the Rice: Phase 2

INGREDIENTS:

2 tablespoons of the oil used to fry the smoked eel

2 ounces cuttlefish, chopped

4½ ounces precooking broth

5½ ounces precooked rice

PREPARATION:

1. With 1 tablespoon of the oil, sauté the diced cuttlefish. Add the broth, and when it boils, add the rice. You'll need to cook this rice for only 4 more minutes for it to be perfectly cooked. During these last few minutes, continuously stir it.

2. To finish, add the 10 grams of remaining oil that will reinforce the eel's smoky aroma, which could have evaporated while cooking.

THE GARNISH

INGREDIENTS:

6 cherries

1 tablespoon rosemary flowers

PREPARATION:

Serve the rice in a deep dish. Finish with 3 cherry halves, the cherry garnish, and the rosemary flowers.

These foods, and the cultural tendency associated with them, of bringing together many loved ones—well, to me that equals happiness.

the icing on the cake
spectacular desserts

Desserts are the weakness of many and the joy of all! If there's one person who knows this well, it's my mother. This wise lady used to tell me that she would give me baklava—a dessert of Arab origin and one of my favorites—if I cleaned my room, did my chores, and behaved. And it works even to this day! I would do anything for baklava.

I believe that every great home chef must have a good variety of recipes to prepare and combine in order to beat the kitchen routine. And the dessert world is so vast! That's why I've included recipes for cake, pudding, tiramisu, crepes, mousse, and many other desserts with common ingredients, and some that you wouldn't even imagine, which will cause quite a sensation, especially if there are children at home. I can tell you from experience that they are the most sincere critics you will find in the kitchen.

Learning how to make desserts is very important in a chef's training because it's one of the cooking areas where you have to be most alert. Here, what I usually say about using recipes as guides, without letting them rule, doesn't really apply, because when it comes to preparing these desserts, success depends on following the recipe very closely. Think about a dessert recipe like a math equation: If you change just one tiny element, the whole equation crumbles. That's why you have to resist the temptation to change little things here and there and to substitute ingredients, because the formula won't be balanced and you could ruin the final outcome.

Now, like everything else in the kitchen, once you start learning and understanding more about baking, you can dare to be more flexible with recipes and make them your own by giving them the touches you desire. And since I want to help you speed up this learning process, I've included a list of general tips that will help you make delicious desserts quickly, sparing you common mistakes and frustrations.

tips to make the best desserts

- It's very important to have utensils in your kitchen that will allow you to accurately measure ingredients. Therefore, I recommend that you use well-calibrated precision scales. If you don't have them at home, they are worth buying! Don't forget to make sure that they read zero before you start weighing ingredients, to avoid any mistakes.

- When it comes to baking, it's very important to follow temperature instructions, but unfortunately, all ovens are different. Therefore, I recommend that you buy a small oven thermometer to help you regulate the temperature according to the recipe's requirements.

- Every time we open a working oven, we let the heat escape quickly, which ends up affecting the cooking temperature and, at the same time, the result of our dessert. Stop yourself from doing this! Try to open the oven only when absolutely necessary.

- It's very important to properly grease baking pans that will go in the oven to bake cakes, using a stick of butter and then adding a couple of teaspoons of flour. After spreading the flour evenly to cover the baking pan, eliminate any excess. The pan should have an even layer of flour covering the inside, which will prevent the cake from sticking to the sides and allow it to rise properly.

- It's important to sift dry ingredients such as flour and sugar through a sieve or colander before including them in the recipes. This will eliminate any lumps and will save you time when mixing.

- Experience has taught me that ingredients usually mix better at room temperature. Therefore, I recommend that you take eggs, milk, butter, or any other ingredient out of the refrigerator a short while before using them. This will guarantee better and easier mixing.

- When you add eggs or egg yolks to a mixture, do it slowly and one at a time. That way you will avoid any lumps or curdling.

- Anytime you have to bake a dessert, place it on the middle rack in the oven unless the recipe indicates otherwise.

- Make sure that both your hands and all the instruments you are going to use are very clean. This includes surfaces where you will be working to prepare your desserts.

- Making desserts is much easier if you have sufficient space, so move whatever you need to be comfortable. You can return everything to its place once you're done.

- Finally, remember to follow recipes closely! Use the correct ingredients in the quantities indicated. I can't stress this point enough. I want to make sure that all of your desserts are extraordinary!

the icing on the cake

chocolate cake

SERVES 8 TO 10

Who doesn't like chocolate? This recipe was inspired by all the amazing chocolate cakes around the world. As a kid, I always wondered how to prepare it at home, and as I learned how to bake, I dedicated myself to making it so that I could satisfy those sweet cravings every now and then. Still, even though the cake always tasted great, after finishing it, I felt something a lot of people feel after indulging in dessert: guilt! For that reason, I've prepared a version that preserves the intense chocolate flavor while making a few adjustments here and there to cut down the calories.

INGREDIENTS:

- 1½ cups flour
- 1½ cups brown sugar
- 1 cup cocoa powder
- 1 tablespoon baking soda
- 2 tablespoons baking powder
- ½ tablespoon salt
- 1 cup milk
- ½ cup olive oil
- 2 eggs
- 1 tablespoon almond extract
- 1 tablespoon orange extract
- ½ cup coffee

FOR THE FROSTING

- ⅓ cup light corn syrup
- 2 tablespoons almond extract
- ⅓ cup brown sugar
- 1 tablespoon orange triple sec liqueur
- 12 ounces semisweet chocolate
- 1 cup heavy cream
- 1 cup raspberries or red blackberries

PREPARATION:

1. Mix the flour, sugar, cocoa powder, baking soda, baking powder, and salt in a bowl.

2. Mix the milk, olive oil, eggs, almond and orange extracts, and coffee in another bowl.

3. Combine the flour mixture and the milk mixture right away with a mixer until smooth. Pour the batter into an ungreased cake pan and bake for about 40 minutes. Remove the cake from the oven and allow to cool.

FOR THE FROSTING

1. In a pot over medium heat, combine the corn syrup, almond extract, brown sugar, and triple sec, and cook until the sugar is dissolved. Let cool.

2. Melt the chocolate in a bain-marie. Add the heavy cream and stir to combine.

3. In a mixer, mix the syrup mixture and the chocolate mixture for 3 minutes.

4. Pour the chocolate icing over the cake.

5. Decorate with the berries.

Desserts are the weakness of many
and the joy of all!

fruit popsicles

SERVES 6 TO 8

I've always been a fan of cold, refreshing, colorful ice pops. One day, while flipping through a wellness magazine, I noticed ice cubes with tiny pieces of fruit and mint frozen inside and I thought, *What a great idea!* So I tried several versions until I got to this wonderful watermelon ice pop recipe. These frozen treats are also perfect to get the little ones at home involved, given how easy they are to prepare.

INGREDIENTS:

> 1 watermelon, cut, seeds removed
>
> 2 tablespoons water
>
> ½ cup sugar
>
> 1 kiwi, cut
>
> 1 orange, cut
>
> 6 sprigs mint
>
> 6 Popsicle molds

PREPARATION:

1. In a food processor, add the watermelon pulp and process until liquid.

2. In a saucepan, add the water and sugar and cook to make a simple syrup. Mix the syrup with the watermelon pulp.

3. In each mold, place a couple of pieces of fruit, 1 fresh mint leaf, and the watermelon pulp, and freeze for about 6 hours.

4. Remove the pops from the molds and serve.

chef james tip >> If you have leftover mix, pour it into an ice tray and freeze. You will soon have flavored ice cubes that you can enjoy on their own, or add to a pitcher of water for flavor.

tres leches bread pudding

SERVES 12

The inspiration for this recipe came from my desire to reinterpret *tres leches* in a simpler way. The difficult part when making *tres leches* is baking the sponge cake. So I decided to use what in the United States we call the poor man's dessert (bread pudding), since it's made with pieces of old bread that are rehydrated with a mixture of egg and heavy cream. When it's combined with the *tres leches* flavor, the result is a delicious dessert.

INGREDIENTS:

1 stick butter

1 pound old bread, cut into 1-inch cubes

2 cups whole milk

1 cup condensed milk

1 cup evaporated milk

1 teaspoon ground cinnamon

10 eggs

1 tablespoon vanilla extract

1 cup vanilla ice cream

PREPARATION:

1. Preheat the oven to 350°F.

2. Use the butter to grease a deep tray and place the bread cubes on the tray.

3. In a bowl, combine the whole milk, condensed milk, evaporated milk, cinnamon, eggs, vanilla extract, and vanilla ice cream, and mix well. Pour the mixture over the bread cubes.

4. Place in the oven and bake for about 35 minutes.

5. Remove the tray from the oven and allow the pudding to sit until it reaches room temperature.

chocolate bread pudding

SERVES 8

This was the first dessert I ever served in my first restaurant, Sabores by Chef James. We used industrial quantities of bread in the restaurant and there was a lot left over. And since I've always been in favor of using everything we have on hand, I decided to include this recipe on our menu. To give it more flavor, I added chocolate chips, which melt a little when warm, and in the mouth of whoever tries this dessert.

INGREDIENTS:

1 stick butter

½ pound brioche

3 eggs

½ cup heavy cream

2 teaspoons vanilla

¼ cup whole milk

½ cup melted dark chocolate

1 teaspoon ground cinnamon

blackberries and blueberries, to decorate

PREPARATION:

1. Preheat the oven to 350°F.

2. Use the butter to grease a heat-resistant glass tray. Cut the bread into cubes and place on the tray.

3. In a bowl, mix the eggs, heavy cream, vanilla, milk, melted chocolate, and cinnamon.

4. Immediately cover the bread with the egg mixture. Press the bread lightly with the palm of your hand. This allows the bread to absorb more of the mixture. Then place the pudding in the oven and bake for 35 to 40 minutes.

5. Allow to sit at room temperature for 30 more minutes, cut, and serve.

chef james tip >> Serve this bread pudding with a scoop of vanilla ice cream to create a contrast between warm and cold.

baked banana s'mores

SERVES 4

My friend Raúl González and I were doing a segment on the television show *Un nuevo día*, preparing this kids' recipe. Everything was ready, we started cooking, and we placed the bananas in the oven. When it was time to remove the bananas from the oven, to my surprise, I saw that the oven was set on high! The result was charred bananas in front of a national TV audience.

I took the classic s'mores and added banana as a binding agent that brings all of it together in a great explosion of flavor. Kids love these s'mores so much that they can be used as a bargaining tool for, say, doing some chores.

INGREDIENTS:

4 bananas

8 tablespoons chocolate chips

4 tablespoons mini marshmallows

1 teaspoon ground cinnamon

6 graham crackers, crumbled

PREPARATION:

1. Preheat the oven 400°F.

2. Using a knife, open a pocket on the peel of each banana. Use a spoon to remove some of each banana's pulp to create space, and fill up the space in each banana with a quarter of the chocolate chips, marshmallows, cinnamon, and graham crackers.

3. Place the filled bananas on a baking tray. Bake until the chocolate and marshmallows melt.

chef james tip >>
The s'mores cook really fast, so keep an eye on them in the oven to avoid burning and experiencing what happened to me on national television! If you want to give this dessert an extra-special touch, serve it with a scoop of vanilla ice cream.

chocolate avocado mousse

SERVES 6

I had to include this version of the popular chocolate mousse, which has fewer calories than the original and is dairy-free, so vegans can enjoy this dessert as well. Though it may be healthier than the usual recipes for chocolate mousse, the flavor tastes just as good. If I could trick a French chef into thinking this was the real thing, you will definitely surprise your guests in the same way. Avocado adds creaminess, but it has a neutral flavor that highlights the chocolate's strength. Also, this dessert is fast and easy to make. The hardest part is waiting for it to cool down in the fridge!

INGREDIENTS:

3 avocados, pitted

½ cup agave nectar

2 tablespoons coconut oil

3 tablespoons granulated sugar

1 tablespoon vanilla extract

1 tablespoon balsamic vinegar

1 tablespoon soy sauce

1 cup cocoa powder

raspberries, to decorate

PREPARATION:

1. Place all ingredients except the cocoa in a food processor and mix until well combined.

2. Add the cocoa and process again.

3. Pour into a large bowl and press the mousse with plastic wrap to set firmly.

4. Place in the refrigerator for 2 hours and serve with raspberries.

chef james tip >> An advantage of this recipe is that you can use avocados that are riper than usual. What you're looking for is their creaminess, so they work perfectly and help you avoid wasting food.

banana and dulce de leche crepes

SERVES 6

This recipe is a lot of fun to prepare because you get to set rum on fire to caramelize the sugar, the procedure called flambé. And it always helps to create somewhat of a spectacle before serving any dish so that guests welcome it with open arms.

INGREDIENTS:

FOR THE CREPES

1 cup flour

1 tablespoon granulated sugar

3 eggs

2 cups milk

2 tablespoons butter

4 tablespoons dulce de leche

TO ASSEMBLE

6 crepes

12 tablespoons dulce de leche

6 tablespoons sugar

6 ounces orange rum

6 scoops vanilla ice cream

PREPARATION:

1. To make the crepes, combine the flour, sugar, eggs, milk, butter, and dulce de leche in a blender and process until uniform.

2. In a 10-inch nonstick pan, ladle enough crepe mixture to spread all over the surface. Allow it to cook, and flip. Repeat with the rest of the batter.

3. To assemble, place 2 tablespoons of dulce de leche on each crepe and fold. Microwave for 1½ minutes and place the crepes on a plate with 1 tablespoon of sugar sprinkled over each crepe.

4. Pour 1 ounce of rum in a glass. Using a lighter, flambé by lighting up the rum and pouring the liquid over the crepe to caramelize the sugar. Repeat with the rest of the crepes.

5. Top each crepe with a scoop of vanilla ice cream.

carrot cake

Just like many other recipes in many other homes, this recipe was passed from generation to generation in my family. It began with my grandmother, who gave it to my mother, who then gave it to me, and now it belongs to all of you. Given the natural sugar found in carrots, we don't need to add that much refined sugar to carrot cake. The magic in this recipe happens in the oven because, as it bakes, the flavors of clove, carrots, and cinnamon combine to create an unparalleled combination. I remember waking up on Sunday mornings and hearing my mom yell: "CARROT CAAAAAAKE," which made me get out of bed immediately.

INGREDIENTS:

- 1 cup agave nectar
- 1 cup olive oil
- 3 eggs
- 2 tablespoons vanilla extract
- 3 cups shredded carrots
- 2 cups flour
- 2 tablespoons baking soda
- 2 tablespoons baking powder
- 2 tablespoons ground cinnamon
- 1 teaspoon ground cloves

PREPARATION:

1. Preheat the oven to 350°F.

2. In a mixer combine the agave nectar, olive oil, eggs, vanilla, and carrots, and blend.

3. In a bowl, combine the flour, baking soda, baking powder, cinnamon, and cloves and sift.

4. With the mixer set at very low speed, gradually add the flour mixture to the carrot mixture.

5. Pour the batter into a cake pan and bake for 45 minutes.

chocolate and banana chimichangas

SERVES 4

Turning a savory food such as chimichangas into a delicious dessert is extremely easy if you use a little bit of imagination and creativity; that's what cooking is all about. When the chocolate melts into the warm banana, the result is an incredible combination in each bite. Be prepared to wipe the chocolate off your lips. I need one right now!

INGREDIENTS:

4 cups canola oil

2 bananas, cut into cubes

½ teaspoon ground cinnamon

½ cup crushed almonds

4 (8-inch) flour tortillas

½ cup hazelnut chocolate spread, plus 1 cup for topping

toothpicks

PREPARATION:

1. Pour the oil into a pot and heat to 350°F.

2. In a bowl, combine the bananas, cinnamon, and almonds.

3. Spread 1 tablespoon of chocolate on each tortilla. Place 2 to 3 tablespoons of banana filling on top of the chocolate and roll the tortilla into a 4-inch rectangle.

4. Hold the tortilla closed with toothpicks and fry in the hot oil until golden.

5. Serve with melted hazelnut chocolate on top to taste.

mango tiramisu

SERVES 4 TO 6

This dessert can be the grand finale of a romantic dinner. Although tiramisu can be a complicated dessert that entails various tedious processes, I found a shorter and simpler way to make it. The things I like the most about this dish are its creaminess and the tropical flavor it gets from the coconut liqueur and mango. This wonderful twist to the traditional Italian recipe has turned this into one of my favorite desserts.

INGREDIENTS:

- ½ cup heavy cream
- ½ cup extra-fine sugar
- ½ cup coconut liqueur
- 1 cup mascarpone
- 2 tablespoons lemon zest
- 4 ripe mangoes
- 1 cup pineapple juice
- 25 ladyfingers

PREPARATION:

1. In a bowl, whip the heavy cream and sugar until stiff. Add 2 tablespoons of the coconut liqueur.

2. Fold the mascarpone and lemon zest into the whipped cream and refrigerate.

3. Blend 2 of the mangoes in a mixer and set aside.

4. Chop the remaining 2 mangoes and set aside.

5. Combine the pineapple juice and the remaining 6 tablespoons of the coconut liqueur in a container.

6. To assemble, place the ladyfingers in the pineapple and liqueur mixture, then place the soaked ladyfingers in a short glass to form a base. Add 2 tablespoons of the whipped cream, followed by the pureed mango, and repeat the process until you get to the rim.

7. Garnish with the chopped mango and mint leaves.

yuca cake

Cassava doesn't get enough credit—it's a really versatile ingredient. It can work as the perfect side dish to barbecues and, as it does here, as the main ingredient of a delicious dessert. Its unique taste and texture make this cake really special. Once you try it, you will never see cassava in the same light again.

INGREDIENTS:

1 pound finely grated cassava

4 tablespoons (½ stick) butter

½ cup sugar

2 eggs

1 teaspoon almond extract

¼ cup evaporated milk

1 teaspoon baking powder

1 teaspoon lemon zest

1 teaspoon orange zest

1 cup blackberry jam

½ cup whipped cream

fresh mint

PREPARATION:

1. Preheat the oven to 350°F.

2. Once you've peeled and grated the cassava, wrap the pulp in a clean kitchen towel and squeeze out the excess liquid.

3. In a glass bowl, mix the butter and sugar until it reaches a creamy consistency. Beat in the eggs and almond extract. Add the evaporated milk, grated cassava, baking powder, lemon zest, and orange zest.

4. Pour the batter into individual round baking dishes and bake for 35 minutes. Remove from the baking dishes and serve with warm blackberry jam, whipped cream, and mint on top.

the icing on the cake

287

natilla

This is a homemade dessert par excellence in all of Latin America. And of course, it comes in several versions. I've included the most delicious and easy to prepare. You would typically see this dessert in December, but the truth is you can prepare it whenever you want, because great flavor is welcome at any time of year!

INGREDIENTS:

4 cups whole milk

1 tablespoon vanilla extract

1 tablespoon cornstarch

4 ounces brown sugar

½ teaspoon baking soda

4 cinnamon sticks

2 tablespoons butter

2 ounces walnuts, chopped

2 ounces almonds, chopped

2 ounces pecans, chopped

PREPARATION:

1. In a saucepan, boil the milk with vanilla. Reduce the heat, add the cornstarch, and dissolve completely. Add the brown sugar and stir until dissolved. Add the baking soda and cinnamon sticks. Stir until the mixture begins to thicken. Cook for about 20 minutes, stirring constantly, until the mixture thickens considerably and the color turns caramel.

2. Remove the cinnamon sticks and add the butter, stirring to combine with the rest of the mixture.

3. Place the custard in a heat-resistant glass container, sprinkle the chopped walnuts, almonds, and pecans on top, cover with plastic wrap, gently pressing the wrap directly onto the custard's surface, and allow to cool for 4 hours.

4. Once it's cooled, cut the custard into cubes and serve.

chef james tip >> To prevent a skin from forming on the top of the custard, cover the surface directly with plastic wrap before cooling.

super churros with guava sauce

SERVES 6 TO 8

This recipe can be the grand finale to any dinner you make at home. Churros, crispy on the outside and soft on the inside, with an intense golden color, are perfect when spread with a delicious guava sauce. The traditional Spanish churro is usually eaten with chocolate or sprinkled with sugar, but I wanted to give this recipe a tropical touch, so I added the guava sauce. Try it at home and tell me which way you like it best!

INGREDIENTS:

FOR THE GUAVA SAUCE
1 cup guava jam
¼ cup water
1 rosemary sprig

FOR THE CHURROS
1 cup water

8 tablespoons (1 stick) butter
¼ cup sugar
1 cup flour
3 eggs
4 cups vegetable oil
¼ cup ground cinnamon, for garnish

PREPARATION:

1. To make the guava sauce, heat the jam with the water and rosemary for 10 minutes.

2. To make the churros, combine the water and butter in a pot and bring to a boil. Add the sugar and stir to dissolve. Add the flour and mix vigorously. Remove from the heat and add the eggs, stirring to combine until the mixture reaches the consistency of dough. Place the dough in a pastry bag with a thick star tip.

3. Form the churros on a tray and refrigerate for about 2 hours.

4. Once they are firm, fry the churros in hot oil until they reach a nice golden color.

> **chef james tip >>** You can cover churros with other sauces to combine more flavors. For example, at my restaurant, Sabores by Chef James, we serve them with 3 sauces: guava, chocolate, and dulce de leche.

happy hour!
surprising cocktails

One of the most entertaining moments in the kitchen happens when we start preparing delicious beverages. Cocktails have been enjoying renewed popularity over the past few years. That's why it's important for any good host to have a variety of quick and easy mixes handy.

Before we dive into the recipes, I want to introduce you to the world of cocktails: their flavors, the most popular liquors, and what types of glasses they should be served in. All of these details will help when it comes time to make them and help you become a memorable host to your guests.

Cocktails are made up of three basic parts: base, body, and aromatic additive, or, as I call it, the aromatic factor. The combination of these three components is responsible for spectacular cocktails or for a not-so-great happy hour that lasts but a few minutes.

- **Base:** A good cocktail depends on a good liquor base, preferably a liquor with an alcohol content between 29 and 60 percent, such as whiskey, brandy, rum, tequila, gin, or vodka.

  The factor that will help us determine the proportion of the base to the rest of the ingredients is the size of the drink. In other words, it depends on whether we are preparing short drinks or tall drinks. In a short drink, especially if it's served in a cocktail glass, the base amount can be somewhere between half and three-quarters of the drink. In tall drinks, the base should make up only about one-quarter of the cocktail's volume. In this case, the liquor flavor is more subtle, although, generally speaking, we will always be able to recognize at least a little of the liquor used for the base.

- **Body:** The body is the ingredient, or the group of ingredients, that complements the flavor and aroma of the base. It could be represented by a liquor that isn't as strong as the base, such as ordinary, sparkling, flavored, or fortified wine, or any other liquid that adds flavor and aroma without significantly increasing the amount of liquor in the drink. It's not a rule, but you will usually find that wine is used in the preparation of short drinks. On the other end of the spectrum, it wouldn't be unusual to see a bartender using champagne to prepare a tall drink.

  As for nonalcoholic ingredients, there are fruit and vegetable juices. They add consistency and sweetness from the fruit, depending on which one you use. Make sure not to overdo it with the sweet liquids if you're counting calories. For a thinner consistency, among the most commonly used juices we find orange juice and blueberry juice, and for a thicker consistency, you could use tomato juice, which is the main ingredient in a bloody mary, one of my favorite drinks. In this book, I share a recipe that will make you fall in love with this drink too!

Other fruit juices commonly used are lime and lemon. Given their acidic flavor, you have to be careful not to add too much of these juices because you could overshadow the flavor of the other ingredients. Also, when using juices, you must remember that, just like with any other ingredient, the quality is very important. We wouldn't want to spoil a delicious cocktail by using a fruit or fruit juice that wasn't at its best.

Other body components are mineral water, sparkling or still, as well as cola-flavored sodas, tonic water, and ginger ale, among others. They all add good flavor and/or sparkling texture to the drink; they are good additions to refreshing drinks.

Finally, a cocktail's body can even be made up of a fatty liquid such as milk or cream, or even the whites and yolk of an egg. A pisco sour, for example, a drink that has gained popularity over the past few years, contains egg whites. Remember that a good cocktail should include these liquids in moderation, because they can make the drink heavy.

> Cocktails have been enjoying renewed popularity over the past few years.

- **Aromatic factor:** The last component in a good cocktail is the aromatic factor! Aromatic additives provide, or highlight, a cocktail's bitter or sweet taste and in some cases even its color. They are divided into syrups and liqueurs, and they can add quite a strong dose of bitterness, as is the case for Campari, although others act mostly as colorants, like in the case of grenadine. Ideally, aromatic factors soften the base liquor's strong flavor and add a new aroma. Some also have the capacity of adding spectacular colors to the drinks, which adds to the aesthetic quality of the overall presentation.

where to serve cocktails

The glass in which you serve a drink is vital to the cocktail's presentation. As crazy as it may sound, this simple detail gives each drink a distinct personality. A James Bond scene at a bar wouldn't be the same without the characteristic martini glass he always holds, and a wine toast among friends wouldn't sound as good without the distinctive wineglass. All of these characteristics make drinks more wonderful and, some might say, even make them taste better.

The truth is, there's an infinite number of glasses in which you can serve cocktails. They vary in size, shape, and even material. Still, you don't need to have them all at home. As long as you have the essential ones, you will be able to serve a great variety of drinks to perfection.

Among the most popular glasses, you will find the following:

- **Wineglasses:** There are two types of wineglasses, one for red wine and one for white. The difference between the two is that the top of the red wineglass is wider so that the wine can breathe. Remember to hold a wineglass by the stem to keep the liquid from changing temperature through contact with your body heat. Finally, when it's time to serve the wine, try not to fill the glass more than halfway.

- **Champagne glasses:** These glasses are longer and narrower than wineglasses. The peculiar shape helps keep the drink's carbonation. These glasses are ideal for bubbling wines as well as for cocktails that include champagne, such as mimosas, Bellinis, and Rossinis.

- **Cocktail glasses:** These glasses have an elegant design and adapt phenomenally to your hand. The top part of a cocktail glass is large to allow room for decorations. Its maximum capacity is 4 ounces, and you will be able to use it to serve the vast majority of cocktails.

- **Martini glasses:** They are used, as the name indicates, to serve martinis in their different versions. This glass is also ideal for serving other cocktails without ice and prepared with vodka. It holds 12 ounces and, just like wineglasses, you have to hold it by the stem to avoid warming up the drink.

- **Highball glasses:** No doubt, one of the most popular glasses used in the cocktail world given its maximum utility, so it is worth having a highball glass at home. It is the glass par excellence to serve "tall drinks" since it allows you to mix several ingredients. Usually, it holds between 8 and 12 ounces.

- **Lowball glasses:** A smaller version of the highball glass, the lowball glass is used mostly to serve drinks on the rocks or cocktails that include distilled liquors among their ingredients. It holds about 6 ounces.

The glass in which you serve a drink is vital to the cocktail's presentation.

Now that you have a better idea of what makes up a cocktail and what to serve it in, you'll have more fun making the cocktails in this book. I have included a selection of original cocktails to encourage you to try all the different mixes and feel more at ease. When you host a family gathering, I want you to be able to surprise your guests with delicious drinks, and there's no doubt in my mind that with these recipes, you will achieve that.

Cheers!

creamy margarita lollipops

SERVES 6 TO 8

This fun drink gives a typical happy hour another dimension in flavor and texture. Creamy margarita lollipops are perfect for surprising and impressing your guests. The inspiration for them came from the idea that we all enjoy food, in one way or another, when it has a fun touch. One day, while sitting with my Sabores creative team, we created a recipe for a lollipop with an interesting twist. After recording it for our YouTube channel, we decided to include it in the menu at Sabores by Chef James. It was a hit for the restaurant, and I guarantee it will be a hit at your next party too!

INGREDIENTS:

juice of 8 lemons

12 ounces condensed milk

1 cup water

½ cup tequila

juice of 1 orange

small plastic cups

wood sticks for lollipops

lemon slices to hold sticks

PREPARATION:

1. Place ingredients in a blender and blend for about 2 minutes, until smooth.

2. Fill each plastic cup with the mixture, place 1 lemon slice on top, and pierce a wooden stick through the lemon slice and halfway into the cup.

3. Set the cups on a platter and place in the freezer for 6 to 8 hours.

passion fruit pisco sour

SERVES 1

Adding passion fruit juice to the classic pisco sour recipe turns it into a drink with a tropical flavor like no other. The best thing about this cocktail is that you can prepare it very quickly and most people really like it, which makes it a good option for any gathering with friends and family.

INGREDIENTS:

2 ounces pisco

1 ounce simple syrup

1 ounce passion fruit juice concentrate

1 egg white

7 ice cubes

ground cinnamon, for sprinkling

PREPARATION:

1. Combine all the ingredients in a blender and blend for 45 seconds.

2. Serve in a short glass or a wineglass, sprinkled with a little bit of cinnamon.

cuban mojito with blueberries

SERVES 1

For this mojito, we add all the flavor and color of delicious blueberries to the classic Cuban drink to give it a touch that will wow your guests. I really like this version because of the great presentation and delicious combination of flavors!

INGREDIENTS:

1 cup blueberries, plus more for garnish

10 leaves fresh mint, plus 1 sprig for garnish

1 ounce sugar

2 ounces lime juice

3 ounces white rum

club soda

PREPARATION:

1. Puree ¾ cup of the blueberries in a blender (add water if necessary).

2. Crush the mint and sugar in a tall glass. Add the lime juice, rum, and blueberry puree.

3. Add ice, then finish the mojito with club soda and stir. Garnish with a mint sprig and some blueberries on a toothpick.

tequila bloody mary

SERVES 1

Being the spice lover I am, it was impossible not to include this delicious cocktail in my book. As opposed to the classic bloody mary, this cocktail replaces vodka with tequila, a liquor that goes incredibly well with the spicy flavor of chiles and hot sauce. It's an absolute delicacy!

INGREDIENTS:

    1 tablespoon pequin chile powder

    1 tablespoon kosher salt

    1 ounce lemon juice

    drizzle of soy sauce

    2 ounces tequila

    3 ounces tomato juice

    drizzle of hot sauce (preferably red)

    1 guajillo chile

PREPARATION:

1. Mix the pequin chile powder and salt on a plate. Wet the rim of a tall glass and rub it with the salt-chile mixture.

2. Add ice to the glass, followed by the lemon juice, soy sauce, tequila, tomato juice, and hot sauce.

3. Mix with a long spoon and garnish with the guajillo chile.

tomatillo bloody mary

SERVES 1

A blender makes this drink very easy and fast to make. This bloody mary version has amazing color and flavor. Get the freshest tomatillos you can find, and if you like the spicy level high, don't be afraid to add a little extra.

INGREDIENTS:

1½ ounces vodka

1 ounce lime juice

1 tablespoon green hot sauce

½ tablespoon prepared spicy radish

1 teaspoon olive juice

1 serrano chile

1 slice lime

4 tomatillos

1 cucumber

1 green apple

1 stalk celery

PREPARATION:

1. Combine all the ingredients except for the celery stalk in a blender, and process until well blended.

2. Strain the mixture to remove the tomatillo, chile, and apple pulp and seeds.

3. Serve in a chilled highball glass and garnish with the celery.

strawberry caipirinha

SERVES 1

Bring all the good flavor of Brazil to your home with this refreshing and delicious strawberry caipirinha. This drink is usually a little sweet, excellent to enjoy during summer days. Try it with your friends and you'll see how they'll want to steal the recipe!

INGREDIENTS:

    6 lemon sections

    2 tablespoons white granulated sugar

    8 strawberry slices

    fresh mint

    1½ ounces cachaça

    ice

PREPARATION:

1. Combine the lemon sections and sugar in a highball glass. Crush the sugar and lemon so that the lemon juice begins to blend evenly with the sugar.

2. Add half of the strawberry slices and crush again.

3. Add the rest of the strawberries and the fresh mint, cachaça, and ice. Mix gently, and enjoy.

espresso martini

SERVES 4

This delicious drink including a dose of caffeine is perfect for any gathering, especially for brunch. I serve it at my restaurant because its unique coffee flavor and, of course, the vodka turned it into a favorite for many. Dare to prepare it at home and look like a professional bartender.

INGREDIENTS:

ice

1 shot espresso coffee

1 ounce vodka

1 ounce coffee liqueur

1 ounce hazelnut liqueur

simple syrup

whipped cream

coffee beans

PREPARATION:

1. Fill a cocktail shaker with ice.

2. Add the espresso, vodka, coffee liqueur, hazelnut liqueur, and simple syrup to taste. Shake vigorously and serve in chilled shot glasses.

3. Top with a generous layer of whipped cream. Then garnish with coffee beans and serve.

light watermelon martini

SERVES 2

For martini lovers, I couldn't leave out this lighter version of the popular cocktail. I daresay it's one of the easiest drinks to make in this book, since the sweet flavor here is provided by the refreshing and colorful watermelon. A very good option if you're counting calories!

INGREDIENTS:

- 3 cups fresh watermelon
- 4 ounces citric or lemon vodka
- juice of 1 lemon
- 2 cups ice
- 2 lemon rings

PREPARATION:

1. Place all the ingredients in a blender and blend for 2 minutes.

2. Serve in martini glasses and garnish with the lemon rings.

sparkling jalapeño margarita

SERVES 1

Margaritas are a refreshing drink to begin with, but with this bubbling version, you'll want them even more, especially in the summer. You'll be surprised at how well the flavor of the jalapeño works with the bubbly champagne.

INGREDIENTS:

2 jalapeño rings

2 tablespoons cilantro leaves

1 ounce orange liqueur

2 ounces lemon juice

2 ounces white tequila

1 ounce gomme syrup

1 ounce champagne

salt, for the glass

PREPARATION:

1. Place the jalapeño rings and cilantro leaves in a glass. Crush gently.

2. Into that same glass, add the orange liqueur, lemon juice, tequila, and gomme syrup. Mix with a spoon to combine well, and add a little bit of ice.

3. Serve in a margarita glass, adding the champagne as the final touch.

traditional sangria

An ideal drink to share with friends during the summer! Its name is derived from its reddish, bloody color (*sangre* is Spanish for "blood"), and it comes from the Iberian Peninsula. It is usually prepared in large quantities and served in a pitcher for everyone to enjoy. The wine used is usually a cheap red, because its flavor is masked by the flavors of the added fruits and other ingredients.

INGREDIENTS:

- 4 tablespoons sugar
- 2 cinnamon sticks
- grated nutmeg
- zest of 1 orange
- 1 liter red wine
- 2 fresh peaches, chopped
- 1 apple, chopped
- 1 pear, chopped
- ½ fresh pineapple, sliced
- 1 orange, sliced
- 2 lemons, sliced
- ½ quart club soda

PREPARATION:

1. In a pot, combine the sugar and 2 tablespoons of water. Immediately add the cinnamon, nutmeg, and orange zest, and heat over medium heat for 10 minutes. Let it cool.

2. In a large pitcher, combine the wine, peaches, apple, pear, pineapple, orange slices, and lemon slices, followed by the soda and the flavored sugar-water syrup.

3. Serve over ice in individual wineglasses.

acknowledgments

I firmly believe that "if you want to walk fast, walk alone; but if you want to walk far, walk with others." My life and my career have been examples of that! I have been fortunate enough to be surrounded by exemplary people who have taken me by the hand to help me get to where I am today, and for that reason, I am eternally grateful to them.

I should start by mainly thanking God for allowing me to do what I love day after day: cooking. I thank him for giving me the opportunity to convey my passion through television, at my restaurant, on social media, and, now, in your own homes through this book. Also, I thank him for giving me the strokes of creativity that allow me to create delicious recipes for everyone every day.

Second, I must thank my big family, especially my mother, a warrior for as long as I can remember, who taught me to always face the world no matter the obstacle, encouraging me to always try to be the best in everything I did. I thank you infinitely for having had the courage to start over in a new country and work so hard to support your children.

I would also like to give a very special thanks to Mr. David, my neighbor and first mentor in the kitchen. I owe him my initiation because he lit the spark and led me to my calling to become a chef. He was the one who developed my palate as a child and taught me a love of cooking. I thank him from here to the sky, where I'm sure he's preparing Galician stew for everyone.

To my grandiose and wonderful work team: Thank you. You are the small giants who have worked tirelessly on this project. I take this moment to thank you for putting your trust in me a few years ago when this project was just starting. That faith in me and in our work made all the difference and allowed this project to grow little by little and get to where we are today. #TeamChefJames

I also have to thank the whole brigade at my restaurant, Sabores by Chef James. Your enthusiasm, determination, and good work are extremely contagious, and they help me immensely to carry on in search of new goals. With all my heart, thank you for being loyal team players!

Also, I must thank the person that gave me the opportunity to start living this dream from which I wish to never wake up: my first television boss and producer, Tony Mojena. I also need to thank and mention the person who had the vision and drive to make me chef at Telemundo: Jesús Becerra, "the black *charro* of Jalisco."

To the people who have taken me by the hand and have contributed tremendously to my career, the M&Ms: María López and Mari García Márquez. Today, I care for you in more than a professional manner, and I will be forever grateful for your help.

To all my chef colleagues who pushed me to stop studying chemistry and study cooking: thank you! Without you, this fantastic career wouldn't have been the same, because you inspired me to be a better chef.

To my friends, who are just a few, but the best! I consider you the family one chooses, and even though there are no blood ties, it hasn't stopped us from loving one another as brothers. Your words, support, and enthusiasm are vital for the growth of all my projects.

And last but not least, I want to give my most heartfelt thanks to everyone who watches the show. Rest assured that without you, *none* of this would've been possible. Thank you for waking up early and tuning in to join me for the morning segment, for looking up recipes online, for sharing on social media, and for being with me day after day. You are always present in my life, and I thank you for walking hand in hand with me on this magical journey!

To all: Thank you for always standing by me, caring for me unconditionally. I have given and will always give you my heart.

for more information

In addition to this book, you can refer to my Web site at www.jamestahhan.com for more inspiration, tips, recipes, or curious facts, as well as on Twitter (@ChefJames), Instagram (@ChefJames), or Facebook.com/chefjamestv.

recipe index